REPRESENTATIONS OF
MARRIAGE AND BEYOND

REPRESENTATIONS OF MARRIAGE AND BEYOND

An Investigation of Early Buddhist Textual Traditions (c.Sixth Century BCE *to Fifth Century* CE*)*

Taniya Roy

PRIMUS BOOKS

PRIMUS BOOKS
An imprint of Ratna Sagar P. Ltd.
Virat Bhavan
Mukherjee Nagar Commercial Complex
Delhi 110 009

Offices at CHENNAI LUCKNOW
AGRA AHMEDABAD BENGALURU BHOPAL COIMBATORE
DEHRADUN GUWAHATI HYDERABAD JAIPUR JALANDHAR
KANPUR KOCHI KOLKATA MUMBAI PATNA RANCHI VARANASI

First published 2022

ISBN: 978-93-5572-125-9 (hardback)
ISBN: 978-93-5572-126-6 (POD)

Published by Primus Books

Laser typeset by Mithu Karmakar
mithu.karma@gmail.com

To

The memories of Maa

Contents

Preface

THIS WORK IS based on my doctoral research that I submitted to the Centre for Historical Studies, Jawaharlal Nehru University, New Delhi, around July 2016. However, my inquisitive mind inculcated and nurtured several issues that altogether evolved the thesis into this monograph.

My experience writing this work would not have been the same without the support and encouragement of several individuals.

First, I am grateful to my mentor Dr Kumkum Roy for her guidance, meticulous attention to details, invaluable comments and immense patience in dealing with the flaws through the years spent in formulating this volume. Without her constant insistence in looking through the diverse possibilities in the sources, many questions would have remained unraised. The entire faculty at the Centre for Historical Studies, Jawaharlal Nehru University, has provided extremely useful insights and suggestions.

I take the opportunity to thank Dr Nupur Dasgupta of Jadavpur University, Kolkata, for introducing me several works of gender historians in the field of social history of early India for the first time during undergraduate lecture classes. My interest in investigating the past of gender relations began there.

Dr Sudeshna Banerjee of Jadavpur University provided an eye-opening look into the everyday practices of ordinary lives. I will always remember her classroom presence in shaping me to look beyond the conventional. I am grateful to late Professor Vijaya Ramaswamy and Professor Mahalakshmi Ramakrishnan for their encouraging words whenever and wherever we met. I thank Dr C. Upender Rao of the Special Centre for Sanskrit Studies at JNU for introducing me to the Pāli language. I am grateful to Professor Ranjan Chakrabarti of Jadavpur University for his constant support and valuable guidance during the formative period of my work.

I am grateful to the librarian and the staff of the Central Library at JNU and the Asiatic Society at Kolkata. My special thanks to late Sunil Babu of DSA library for all his assistance in the formative period of the thesis.

My friends, my cousins and all my well-wishers will always be remembered for their affection and support and for bearing with all my moods.

Finally, I thank my father for our endless discussions that aroused my interest in social issues. There can be no words to acknowledge his immense indulgence, encouragement and trust. Thank you, Baba, for letting me be myself and do whatever I want. Nothing would have been possible without your reassurances in times of every crisis I faced. I thank Maa for her omnipresence and blessings despite her bodily absence.

Lastly, I thank the Almighty for everything.

Kolkata — TANIYA ROY

Introduction

MARRIAGE IS ONE of the most important institutions in the Indian subcontinent. This rite initiates an individual into the life of a householder. This stage of life is defined by the individual's worldly duties and production of offspring. Richard Gombrich[1] poses a contrast between communal or social religions and those emphasizing soteriology. He states that soteriology would not regard nuptial ties as more significant than initiation to the religion. It is evident from Buddhist texts that the Buddha preached soteriology and Buddhism was regarded as a heterodox religious sect that rose in the background of the sixth century BC in the Ganga valley as a critique of the Vedic and other brāhmaṇical religions. However, the Buddha was no reformer. He never denied the existing caste system nor attacked the patriarchal misogyny of society. Rather, he tried to show an alternative system of salvation which was beyond gender bias, and which could be followed without giving much importance to the caste system or Vedic rituals.

This seems to be true of the Buddhist attitude towards marriage. We hardly find depictions of marriage rites in early Buddhist texts but marriage is still the linchpin of narratives in the Buddhist textual traditions. It is difficult to treat the Buddhist traditions as completely antithetical to the life of the householder. Maximum assistance for the sustenance of the saṇgha came from the lay supporters. It might be possible that Buddhist texts, instead of regarding marriage and soteriology as antithetical to each other, perceived liberation as an aspect beyond the worldly existence of the individual in society. Renunciation was an alternative to all the sufferings generated from worldly ties.

While some scholars think that the written narratives contain only partial truths and are coloured by the predispositions of the authors, there are various interpretive mechanisms that open up immense possibilities. Since this study of the aspects of marriage is based on the understanding of the Buddhist texts, it is imperative to highlight the method that will be adopted in the treatment of the texts in the present work.

Here, the analysis of various aspects of nuptial ties and what lay beyond them are based on the study of Buddhist narratives—primarily the birth stories of the Buddha as presented in the Jātakas, the songs of the nuns (*therīs*) as compiled in the *Therīgāthā* and the verses of the monks (*theras*) as represented in the *Theragāthā*. I will examine both the specificities of these texts as well as their intertextuality. With the belief that textual representations can systematize social imagery common to a society as observed by the authors, an enquiry will be made into the texts and their representations.

Sources and Questions

The three selected textual traditions, the Jātakas, *Therīgāthā*, and *Theragāthā* are broadly representative but are not unanimous in their treatment of marriage and relations based on it. One important observation that arises out of the study of these texts is the fact that they were not penned by any single author. Instead, these texts evolved over time. A significant trend of this literary genre of the Buddhist Pāli canon was the organization of the *bhāṇakas* (Buddhist monks who recited specific collections of texts) who recited these texts. K.R. Norman refers to the *Khuddaka bhāṇakas*, who had profound knowledge about the history of early Buddhism.[2] It can be said that in the long period of the composition of the texts the oral narratives might not have been entirely in Pāli. The languages spoken by different *bhāṇakas* may have formed a significant part in the medium of the composition. It was after the demise of the Buddha that councils decided to compile the canonical literature in lingual uniformity. Thus, Pāli became the language of the Buddhist canonical texts. The Tripiṭakas underwent a threefold division and a fivefold division becomes operative for the Nikāyas (collection/subdivisions within the Tripiṭakas).[3] There is a basic trait of these texts adhering to the Buddhist ethos—they are vibrant and have a life of their own. The rationale behind the selection of each of the texts for enquiring into certain social aspects of marriage and understanding assumptions beyond the institution of marriage is discussed below.

Why the Jātakas?

Intensive work on the structure of the Jātakas, from a historical perspective, has been done by Uma Chakravarti[4] and Kumkum Roy[5] in the recent past. Based on their work, I will discuss the chronological uncertainties of the text. It has been argued by Roy that the text was composed and compiled over several centuries. She explored inscriptional and sculptural evidence[6] (for example, the scenes from the Jātakas engraved on the entrance of the Sanchi stupa) and assigned the circulation of many of the stories to the third century BCE while a compiled form may be dated to the fifth century CE.[7]

The narratives were in oral form and were an important part of the folktale genre in the Indian subcontinent. The written form that we find today encompasses a huge list of more than 540 stories, divided into the story of the present birth of the Buddha (*paccupannavatthu*), the story of the past births of the Buddha (*atītavatthu*), the canonical section (*gāthā*) and the last section called *samodhāna*, where the Buddha identifies the characters of the past and present narratives.[8]

To some extent the 'sacred but not sacrosanct'[9] status assigned to this particular textual genre by Roy seems dubious. In the face of the inclusion of the everyday lives of common folk as well as being subject to interpolation, the sacred status of the Jātakas is questionable. It might be possible that the text was subjected to regular recitation, highlighting the common problems of individuals and possible solutions through a reliance on the Buddhist ethos. The audience included masses from different classes and castes of society. We can hardly be assured of the unanimous status of the Buddha and his philosophy as sacred to them. Yet, simple and mundane solutions advocated in Buddhist philosophy were attractive. In other words, perhaps the Buddha was not a sacred figure to many but he was a popular persona. Thus, the stories were given an extremely popular status, which often happens with parables and fables. The canonical status gained by the Jātakas in the later period, as mentioned by K.R. Norman, was due to its inclusion in the Pālī *Khuddaka Nikāya.* This primarily indicates the Buddhist religious purposes served by it in popularizing the wisdom gained by the Buddha in different birth cycles.[10]

Indeed, the representations of the day-to-day experience of the masses become a potent ground for investigating the Jātakas to locate the varied aspects of the institution of marriage. The use of the animal motif in the narratives draws much attention. It functions in a very palpable way to replicate the human world. The hierarchical divide of the human world between the rich and poor, the dutiful man and his suspicious wife, and the vigilant pet over a licentious woman becomes apparent. Marriages conducted between partners of different status were not the norm and this reflects in narratives where an animal belonging to a high status like a lion or a tiger could never befriend a jackal (which was considered low status). However, we hardly find examples of animal motifs being used to describe the asocial world of renunciation. The narratives describing the different births of the Buddha are borrowed extensively across traditions but given a Buddhist twist.

Why the Therīgāthā?

The reasons for selecting the *Therīgāthā* as a source for the present work are numerous. K.R. Blackstone argues that the *Therīgāthā* is a provocative text and affirms female authorship to it. Since these texts record the verses of the *therīs* in their transition phase, we are given glimpses of their past lives as wives, daughters, mothers, courtesans, etc. The same can be said for the *Theragāthā*.[11] Like the Jātakas, the commentary on the *Therīgāthā* and the *Theragāthā* contextualizes the verses.

The name and the social background of the 'author' form crucial elements of the verses in the *Therīgāthā*. This is followed by the portrayal of the circumstance under which the *therī* accepted Buddhism.[12] Tracing the chronological structure of the *Therīgāthā*, Blackstone suggested that the text developed over several centuries spanning the sixth to the end of the third century BCE. The *Therīgāthā* is mainly in verse; the *gāthās* are embedded in a prose commentary, the *Paramatthadīpanī*, composed in Kanchipuram in the sixth century CE and attributed to a monk named Dhammapāla.[13] It contains a total of 522 verses compiled into 73 poems. It is likely, as Charles Hallise, suggests, that some of the verses were composed during the time of the Buddha.[14]

Studying the nature of the text, it becomes clear that the subject matter varied from hardships in the past life of the *therīs* to the influence of other renouncers and also to a sincere quest for liberation from worldly sufferings. The alternative arrangement in the saṇgha (as opposed to married life) as portrayed in the verses makes it interesting. Women could actually thrive in the saṇgha without the constraints of patriarchal norms. Besides the varied alternatives in the saṇgha, the erudite *bhikkhunīs* demand most of the attention. Roy compared the position of a learned *bhikkhunī* Dhammadinnā with her brāhmaṇical counterpart Gārgī. Fascinatingly, in the Buddhist tradition, Dhammadinnā has been acknowledged as a teacher unlike Gārgī in the *Bṛhādaraṇyaka Upaniṣad.*[15]

Most importantly, these verses allow us to listen to the rebellious voices of women in a patriarchal society where they affirmed in their verses that they did not want a life of household chores and drudgery; instead, they wanted to be learned in the Buddha's wisdom.

Why the Theragāthā?

Since this work mainly focuses on gender relations in the textual traditions, a study of the *Theragāthā* is important as an analysis of these verses is necessary in order to grapple with the gender difference in the experiences of men and women in both the social and asocial worlds. The compilation of 1279 verses are arranged into poems and divided into *nipātas* (subdivision of texts). As in the case of the *bhikkhunīs*, not all the verses were authored by the concerned *bhikkhus*; at times certain verses are addressed to them.

Norman suggests that many of the verses in the *Theragāthā* are descriptions of the *theras*' attempts to attain liberation. Some are merely verses of a general nature, while in others the description of their personal lives and accounts of nature is clear. Norman also mentions the secular aspect of some of the verses where descriptions of nature are widespread which is followed by the description of the *thera*'s religious quest.[16]

Ideological Location of the Early Buddhist Textual Traditions

Stephanie Jamison's statement—'in a field in which affixing a date to a text or a concept (even a vague date spanning several centuries) is an act of daring'[17]—becomes relevant in the study of the social background of the period for texts which were compiled over several centuries. The time span for this work is approximately the sixth century BCE to the fifth century CE. This period witnessed far-reaching changes in political, material and social life. The major powers ruling across this stretch of time rangded from territorial polities in the form of the *mahājanapadas*, the Haryaṅka dynasty of Magadha, the Śiṣunāgas, the Nandas, the Mauryas, the successor dynasties and others followed by the Guptas.

The greater part of northern India witnessed urbanization during this period. As a result, the Ganga valley perceived the complexities of socio-economic life as being associated with urban development. The shift from the productive system of communal ownership of land under the *gaṇasaṇgha* (collective ownership of land) to the private ownership of land by the *gahapati* (wealthy householder engaged in agriculture) was a significant social transition. With technological innovations inaugurated at the beginning of the Iron Age in northern India, the old agrarian social order underwent a dramatic transformation.

A new sense of individuality emerged, especially among those located along the social and spiritual margins of the prevailing brāhmaṇical culture. In the newly emerging social climate, women had adequate scope to express their religious inclinations.[18] No less significant was the advent of new religious groups that challenged the infallibility of the Vedas. Foremost amongst them were Buddhism and Jainism.[19] This was because Buddhism maintained a basic concern for the economic development of the time while advocating sincerely for *nibbāna* (nirvana) as a noble path.

Chakravarti in her essay, 'The Social Philosophy of Buddhism',[20] suggests that gender relations were much altered in the changing economy. Controlling the chastity of women became a priority in order to guarantee legitimate succession in a patrilineal kinship system. Adultery became a threat to patriarchy in a changing society. The function of women was reduced to producing legitimate heirs for the family. Chakravarti states that the constant representation of the need to police women makes it clear that women may have resented the role of 'good wife' imposed on them.

Romila Thapar in a section entitled 'Alternative Histories' in her recent work[21] discussed the Buddhist way of constructing the past and forming historic traditions. She regards the Buddha as a historical person, whose life has been visualized by the Buddhists as a benchmark in history. Thus, his teachings were given a canonical structure by his disciples. She mentioned that the Buddha approved of a clan-based oligarchical form of government, and his teachings were primarily in the urban context.

Buddhist religion developed in different forms in various regions of the Indian subcontinent. In the northern plain, where Buddhism originated, the religion was not prevalent in an institutionalized form; instead; it developed at a level of individual patronage. This was in contrast to the development of Buddhism in other parts of India where the religion was institutionalized. If historical tradition can be conceived as the perception of the past, then the reason for the change in Buddhism at different periods of history can be located in a historical context. Buddha was contemporary to the rise of the *ganasaṇgha*; he had the authority to rule but developed spiritual leadership. In the early Pali canon, the Buddhist ethos was formulated to be in sync with the society at large. Contemporary society was experiencing a rise of heterodox traditions as alternatives to rigid conventional norms. The ground was already prepared for the acceptance of an alternative religious route. The middle path propagated by the Buddha was, thus, in sync with a society that was no longer ready to comply with the increased rigidity of brāhmaṇical religion. This social conflict and its negotiations and contestations are the subjects of many narratives in the Jātakas, the *Therīgāthā*, and the *Theragāthā*. The intention of each of the texts studied here is to make sense of the social history of the contemporary period in which it germinated. Since the focus of my work here is to trace the past of gender relations, the understanding of this social background is significant in the analysis of gender relations as evident in the textual representations. Although the authenticity of the texts used here are not certain, their historical consciousness cannot be ignored.

Historiographical Issues

So far, we have hardly come across any comprehensive works focusing on the portrayal of marriage in early Buddhist textual traditions. Yet, there are ample references to gender relations in the works of different scholars. Chakravarti[22] recognized early Buddhist attempts to establish new production relations and their vehement opposition to the brāhmaṇical claim to inherent status. The Buddha also disapproved of the brāhmaṇical attempt to exercise rights over land grants by kings. Chakravarti points out that the disapproval was operational due to the fact that if brāhmaṇas had rights over the means of production it would be difficult to deny their superior status in the social hierarchy. She also discusses the reference to endogamy in the Buddhist texts. In the context of marriage, jāti was of great significance. Importantly, her observation on the Buddhist textual evidence explicated the fact that the Buddhists' way of establishing new production relations with the *gahapati* in a superior position probably did not succeed. Therefore, a feasible alternative to the brāhmaṇical system could not materialize. Thus, endogamy was prevalent in marriages but the essential link between endogamy, occupation-based identity and inherent claim to higher status was not visible. She suggested that all these elements were linked with the *varṇasaṃkara* theory (mixed-caste theory, as opposed to endogamy) in a complex production system based on endogamy at the jāti level for the smooth functioning of the social structure.

Gerda Lerner[23] emphatically argued that the concept of gender must be analysed historically keeping in mind its specificity in changing societies. She challenged the biologically determinist theories of traditionalists as immature, and, by nullifying the 'man the hunter' statement as inadequate, she agreed with other feminist anthropologists contesting the assumption of the natural-given superiority of men.

Kirit K. Shah stated that 'the concept of gender calls for rewriting of all history seeking historical space for the missing half of humanity, destressing the concern with social and economic history and pleading a place as much for the general as for the unique.'[24]

One of the most significant works on the social relations between the sexes is found in Chakravarti's renowned work *Everyday Lives, Everyday Histories*.[25] She analysed how the protection of female chastity in the changing economy of the time period covered became a much-valued social concern. Chakravarti recognized the obsession of preventing adultery by one's wife as an urgent necessity in the patrilineal kinship system. The relations of production against the new social background provided the base in which relations between the sexes crystallized into permanent institutions. She reflected on the awareness of the Buddha regarding the unequal positioning of women in gender relations and stated that the Buddha, despite acknowledging the inherent discrimination between the sexes, didn't reject it. This becomes evident in the all-pervasive inequality in the Buddhist saṇgha.

Chakravarti's unique handling of the stories of the Jātakas, in her article 'Women, Men and Beasts: The *Jātaka* as Popular Tradition' is useful in understanding the gendered world in everyday lives as evident in the Buddha's birth legends. She pointed out that in the Jātaka stories the husband-wife 'dyad' was always portrayed negatively. Alan Sponberg implies a fresh approach in his study that breaks the stereotyped perception of the existing historiography. In his work[26] 'Attitudes Towards Women and the Feminine in Early Buddhism', he perceived the existence of the negative attitude towards women as portrayed in Buddhist texts from a different viewpoint, focusing on the heterogeneous and open-ended nature of Buddhist traditions. Sponberg states that there are underlying tensions within Buddhist literature—a tension between certain attitudes that seem unusually positive in the assessment of women, and feminism and attitudes that are more negative on the other hand. Moti Chandra's argument[27] regarding the courtesans of Buddhist literature is also significant. He said that compared to the *gaṇikās* (courtesans) in the *Arthaśāstra*, their counterparts in the Buddhist texts are described as an affluent class. They were marked by their glamorous existence and were well known for charging hefty amounts from their clients. Their clients included not only kings but anybody with wealth. Chandra mentioned a number of synonyms used for courtesans—*vesī*, *nāriyo*, *gaṇikā*, *nagarasobhanī*, *vaṇṇadāsī*, and *kumbhadāsī*—in the Jātakas, which indicated the wide prevalence of sex work in the social sphere. He mentioned that these synonyms might be indicative of the hierarchical status in the profession.

A few works that questioned the assumptions of earlier historical writings have also been produced. One of the most significant works on gender relations as represented in textual traditions in early India has been Roy's study *The Power of Gender and the Gender of Power.*[28] She explored the Jātakas, the *Therīgāthā*, and the *Theragāthā* in this work. She focused on each text from multiple perspectives, interrogating and analysing the pervasive misogyny of the Buddhist texts. Roy focused on the terrain of adultery from an analytical perspective, exploring how the treatment of adultery was far from a homogeneous phenomenon. The mode of punishment for this crime hardly remained constant. She mentioned how the treatment of the adulterous king varied from that of a queen through the analysis of the Jātaka stories. Roy, in her article 'Recent Studies on Gender Relations in Early India', stated that the analysis of gender relations requires us to be sensitive towards the hindrance of generalizations often made about gender norms in society. Rather, she asks readers to take into consideration the varied social contexts that gave rise to such gender norms. She points out the significance of the intersections of caste, class and cultural traditions in the understanding of these categories of men and women.[29]

In her monograph, Blackstone[30] made a comparative study on the *Theragāthā* and *Therīgāthā* and tried to analyse the gendered aspect of liberation. In the chapter entitled

'The Language of Liberation', she highlighted the inherent differences between the two texts. Interestingly, she pointed out that the *Theragāthā* is more author-oriented than the *Therīgāthā* and focuses on the *thera* himself and his attainment of nirvana, whereas the *Therīgāthā* appears to focus on the *therīs*' past experiences in order to contextualize her path to liberation; her past lives and social roles are often the main themes of the work. Blackstone's work created an impression in asserting female authorship to the *Therīgāthā*.

John G. Jones[31] provides a thematic discussion on gender relations in Buddhist textual traditions. In the chapter 'Sex and Marriage: Love and Friendship', he analysed the inherent misogyny in the Jātakas and contextualized it in a meaningful way. He pointed out that the Jātakas' objection to marriage is beyond theoretical and stated that the objections are based on anecdotes about the practical disadvantages and disillusionments of the married state. He also mentioned that there are stories which persist in presenting the married state in a much more favourable light than found in the Nikāyas.

The work of Meena Talim[32] explored different women with common characteristics and the characteristic features of their lives. In one section Talim dealt with women's contribution to the development of the life of the Bodhisatta. There, she referred to instances from the Jātaka tales to show how women played an important role in developing the supreme personalities of the Bodhisattas.

Rita M. Gross[33] argued that many of the Mahāyāna texts deemed womanhood and buddhahood as antithetical to each other. She also talked about another possibility, where buddhahood stood beyond the gendered paradigm. However, the inclusion of women and the feminine in Vajrayāna Buddhism was a later development. She argued that classical Buddhism can be defined as androcentric in its thought as it wanted to exclude women from religious pursuits and leadership roles. Classical Buddhism was patriarchal in its institutions as certain rules were set for the ordination of nuns which confirmed their innate subordination to the monks. Gross said that Buddhism was androcentric and patriarchal but not highly misogynistic.[34]

Alice Collett expressed the need to shift away from the prevailing view in Buddhist narratives of female sexuality as voracious.[35] She explored the divergent sexuality in the *saṇghādisesa* rules (rules for Buddhist monks) of the Pāli Vinaya (collection of different monastic rules). She tried to look into the nuances of female sexuality as referred to in the Pali canon, commented upon by male voices. Women are commonly depicted as enticers of men and imagined to be born with inbuilt traits of licentiousness. Collett found that certain set of rules in the Vinaya indicated that men actively sought sex and women need to be aware of the potential danger of male sexuality and remain alert of the same. She also allowed us to look at the instances of mutual consent and examples of active and healthy male and female desire. There are also instances where women responded to the idea that offering sex to monks was the highest mode of gifting as laywomen.

Amy Langenberg's essay[36] critically questioned the social position of the nun. Her study revealed that the Indian Buddhist nun stood at the crossroads of womanly virtue expected of a laywoman and a female ascetic. She analysed the *Mahāsāṇghika-Lokottaravādin Bhikṣuṇī Vinaya* that recorded selected roles of Buddhist monks and nun and functions available to respectable women in order to construct a public identity for nuns that neither resisted telling nor repelled the donations and opinion of the laity. She believed that the nun-centric Vinaya was useful as a guide for *Mahāsāṇghika-Lokottaravādin* nuns in their negotiation of complex and sometimes hostile social environment. The study also suggests that the social vulnerability of Buddhist nuns is a consequence not simply of their public image as unguarded females of questionable virtue but also from the fact that they attempted to occupy a frontier position at the intersection of two well-established social identities—that of a virtuous woman and a Buddhist ascetic. The *Mahāsāṇghika-Lokottaravādin Bhikṣuṇī Vinaya* is unique and has been edited to present a comprehensive set of rules to address this vulnerable position.

Bhikkhu Anālayo studied the ten discourses found in a collection of texts called Saṃyukta-āgama, preserved in a Chinese translation where *bhikkhunīs* are the protagonists.[37] He analyses the role of Māra (representation of the evil side of humanity)[38] who appears in all ten discourses. Considerable body of scholarly literature on Māra explains the symbolic significance which has been reconstructed by Bhikkhu Anālayo. A close analysis of textual evidences brings forth that unlike the *bhikkhus*, *bhikkhunīs* never failed to recognize the evil Māra. This reflects the fact the *bhikkhunīs* are arhants (Buddhist monks who have achieved nirvana) and could be compared to their male counterparts, who evidently could not reach the same level of perfection. What is notable is the fact in contrast to the early Buddhist literature, the ten sets of discourses analysed by Bhikkhu Anālayo clearly hints at the favourable position of *bhikkhunīs*.

V. Geetha explains that it is common to invoke tradition to justify a social norm.[39] People in a given context perceive themselves on the basis of the norms that regulate male and female behavior and set limits for what might be permitted for men and women in a given social context. She also emphasized the role of tradition and religion in regulating the life of people. These norms are not always present in codified form but are omnipresent as ideas and notions that regulate the everyday life of common folk.

The Outline of the Study

This work was conceived as a study of gender relations in the context of marriage as a social institution organized by caste, class or social strata, gender norms and the intervention of the Buddha in resolving conflicts. It was premised on the postulation that the narratives of the Jātakas, the *Therīgāthā* and the *Theragāthā* could provide ideal material to probe into questions related to such an enquiry. Texts of this magnitude have never been examined in the paradigm of marriage and its related aspects. The social imaginary—which is a set of values, institutions and meanings common to a particular society as experienced by a social subject—is a matter of concern in each of the narratives and verses discussed here. Given the fact that these narratives are not homogenous and are broadly open-ended in nature, my engagement with the Buddhist textual tradition is varied. The goal is not to deal with the hermeneutical aspect of the texts but to focus on the social norms and conventions that enable the understanding of history. The aim of this volume is strictly to write a past of gender relations. The historiographical study made earlier situates the present work within the study of human relations and other social aspects.

In discussing the literature concentrating on the social aspects of Buddhism and gender relations in Buddhist literature we will explore a range of issues concerning the sociology of heterodox sects in general and Buddhism in particular. We will observe how caste always remained a foundational question in the realm of matrimonial relations.

Chapter 1 begins with the portrayal of marriage and its varied aspects in Buddhist texts. The representation of marriages in the concerned Buddhist texts will be examined through specific questions. Whether the conceptual caste structure was a mere continuation or underwent a change during the Buddha's time will also be discussed. I will investigate how choice and consent actually operated in negotiating matrimonial alliances.

In Chapter 2 the understanding of the idea of social relations beyond marriage will be explored through the examination of variations in nuptial ties. For instance, representations of *anuloma* and *pratiloma* marriages juxtaposed against the ideal form of endogamous marriage are notable. In this chapter, the working of marriages between partners will be studied. This will allow us to locate the construction of 'proper' and 'improper' in the Buddhist way of understanding the society in which the institution developed.

Chapter 3 will discuss the various facets of matrimonial alliances among householders. The Buddhist ethos regards the household of the social world as the harbinger of suffering; the antidote to this lies in renouncing social life in the quest of liberation. In this context the gendered nature of the household will be analysed by examining the structural paradigm of the household. The rituals and traditions tied to the spatial identity of the household have a gendered identity, which will be studied here. Marriages that were intrinsically related to begetting offspring might not have given equal right to both the partners over their progeny. The relation of dependence resting on structural relations in the household will be closely examined. This may lead us to to perceive what is meant by 'beyond' in the spatial understanding of a nuptial tie.

In the final chapter (Chapter 4), the holistic purview of worldly suffering that sprang out of nuptial ties will be juxtaposed against the significant notion of renouncing the social world. This will enable us to arrive at a contrasting overview of the representation of marriage and renunciation. The consent of the individual in his/her admission to the

Buddhist order as a close parallel (or as an alternative) to the representation of marriage will be analysed.

This work attempts a comparative analysis of evidence to examine the significance of the notion of caste, class and gender variables in the understanding of matrimonial alliances in the Buddhist textual tradition in particular and renunciation in general. The study of the close association of gender and caste is the basic foundation in analysing the evidence of social development as perceived in the Jātakas, the *Therīgāthā* and the *Theragāthā*. The main focus of this work remains the representation of the diverse aspects of marriages and an understanding of what is 'beyond' this institution through textual evidences. I will also try to understand the scope of liberation in negotiating and challenging the complexities of worldly life.

NOTES

1. Richard F. Gombrich, *Theravāda Buddhism*, London and New York: Routledge, 2006, p. 27.
2. K.R. Norman, *A History of Indian Literature: Pālī Literature*, Wiesbaden: Otto Harrassowitz, 1983, p. 9.
3. Ibid., p. 15.
4. Uma Chakravarti, *Everyday Lives, Everyday Histories: Beyond the Kings and Brahmanas of 'Ancient' India*, New Delhi: Tulika Books, 2006.
5. Kumkum Roy, *The Power of Gender and the Gender of Power: Explorations in Early Indian History*, New Delhi: Oxford University Press, 2010.
6. This evidence allows us to guess the time period in which certain stories flourished. It has to be noted that the Jātaka stories actually developed and evolved over time. That makes ascertaining of exact chronology and authorship difficult. However, the compiled form in which we find the Jātakas today is a much later development.
7. Roy, *The Power of Gender*, p. 115.
8. Ibid., p. 290.
9. Ibid., p. 291.
10. Norman points out that the *Dīgha-bhāṇakas* and the *Majjhima-*

bhāṇakas excluded the *Khuddaka Nikāya* from their list of canonical texts, which probably means that it had not yet attained canonical status at the time when their lists were closed. See Norman, *A History of Indian Literature*, p. 57.

11. K.R. Blackstone, *Women in the Footsteps of the Buddha: Struggle for Liberation in the Therigāthā*, New Delhi: Motilal Banarsidass, 2000, p. 2.
12. Roy, *The Power of Gender*, p. 18.
13. Ibid., pp. 2–3.
14. Charles Hallisey, tr., Introduction to *Therīgāthā: Poems of the First Buddhist Women*, London: Murty Classical Library of India, 2015, p. x.
15. Kumkum Roy, *Gender and Early Textual Traditions*, Trupunithura, Kerala: Govt. Sanskrit College, 2015, p. 27.
16. Ibid., pp. 74–5.
17. Stephanie W. Jamison, 'Women "Between the Empires" and "Between the Lines"', in *Between the Empires: Society in India 300 BCE to 400 CE*, ed. Patrick Olivelle, New York: Oxford University Press, 2007, p. 191.
18. Alan Sponberg, 'Attitudes Toward Women and the Feminine in Early Buddhism', in *Buddhism, Sexuality and Gender*, ed. Jose Ignacio Cabezon, New Delhi: Sri Satguru Publications, 1992, p. 45.
19. Ranabir Chakravarti, *Exploring Early India: Upto c.AD 1300*, New Delhi: Primus Books, 2016, p. 83.
20. Uma Chakaravarty, 'The Social Philosophy of Buddhism', in *Everyday Lives, Everyday Histories: Beyond the Kings and Brahmanas of 'Ancient' India*, New Delhi: Tulika Books, 2006, p. 124.
21. Romila Thapar, *The Past Before Us: Historical traditions of Early North India*, New Delhi: Permanent Black, 2013.
22. Uma Chakravarti, *Gendering Caste through a Feminist Lens*, Kolkata: Stree, 2006, pp. 46–9.
23. Gerda Lerner, *The Creation of Patriarchy*, New York: Oxford University Press, 1986, p. 37.
24. Kirit K. Shah, ed., *History and Gender: Some Explorations*, New Delhi and Jaipur: Rawat Publications, 2005, pp. 1–2.
25. Chakravarti, *Everyday Lives Everyday Histories*, pp. 204–8.
26. Sponberg, 'Attitudes Towards Women', pp. 3–5.
27. Moti Chandra, *The World of Courtesans*, New Delhi: Vikas, 1973, p. 23.
28. Roy, *The Power of Gender.*

29. Kumkum Roy, 'Recent Writings on Gender Relations in Early India', in Shah, ed., *History and Gender*, p. 89.
30. Blackstone, *Women in the Footsteps of the Buddha*, p. 24.
31. John G. Jones, *Tales and Teachings of the Buddha*, USA: Cyber Editions, pp. 72–4.
32. Meena Talim, *Woman in Early Buddhist Literature*, Mumbai: University of Bombay, 1972, pp. 14–15.
33. Rita M. Gross, *Buddhism after Patriarchy: A Feminist History, Analysis, and Reconstruction of Buddhism*, New Delhi: Sri Satguru Publications, 1995.
34. Ibid., p. 30.
35. Alice Collett, 'Pāli Vinaya: Reconseptualising Female Sexuality in Early Buddhism', in *Women in Early Indian Buddhism: Comparative Textual Studies*, ed. Alice Collett, New York: Oxford University Press, 2014.
36. Amy Paris Langenberg, 'Mahāsāṇghika-Lokottaravāda Bhikṣuṇī Vinaya: The Intersection of Womanly Virtue and Buddhist Asceticism', in Collett, ed., *Women in Early Indian Buddhism.*
37. Bhikkhu Anālayo, 'Saṃyutta-nikāya/Saṃyukta-āgama: Defying Māra-Bhikkhunīs in the Saṃyukta-Āgama' in Collett, ed., *Women in Early Indian Buddhism.*
38. Māra is a personification of the evil side of the human mind that often thwarts progress and causes spiritual upheaval. In Buddhist narratives, Māra appears in different forms and plays various roles to malign human characters in their everyday lives. Often, in descriptions of conjugal life, Māra appears to provide tough challenges; however, these challenges are always superseded by following the Buddha's teachings.
39. V. Geetha, *Patriarchy*, Kolkata: Stree, 2009.

1

Marriage as Negotiation and Contestation

THE EARLY BUDDHIST textual traditions (the Jātakas, the *Therīgāthā*, and the *Theragāthā*) were conceived in a period of transition (*c.*sixth century BCE to fifth century CE) that witnessed both change and continuity. These popular texts of the Buddhist tradition offer a closer inspection of the institution of marriage which formed an important part of the social world, as it provided a ground for production and reproduction (as children eventually became *prajas* and played a role in the economic transition of society). Given that the Buddhist ethos functioned on the high value assigned to the renunciation of worldly ties, the urge to contemplate the representation of matrimonial ties in the Buddhist texts has a distinct rationale. The key to the understanding of gender relations and marriage in Buddhist literature lies in a synchronic approach. Although the portrayal of marriage rituals is absent in Buddhist textual traditions, the descriptions of negotiations and contestations in relation to marital ties are omnipresent. The status of the concerned individuals often played a determining role in marriages. These experiences were frequently gendered and, thus, demand scrutiny.

The canonical literature hardly has anything good to say about attachment. Words like *mettā* (love) and *karuṇā* (compassion) often occur in a general sense and have nothing to do with attachments common to marriage or friendship.[1] The Jātakas quintessentially describe marriage as an institution that generates numerous problems. A situation of disadvantage has been constantly represented in the portrayal of the married life of an individual. However, a few narratives in the Jātakas represent marriage in a favourable light. One can deduce the prominent influence of the lay audiences in shaping those stories as the Jātaka narratives evolved over time, where the everyday lives of the common folk or lay audiences played an important role in determining their course.

The potential of an alternative to worldly sufferings (often represented in the life of a householder) was manifested in the saṇgha and we encounter this in the verses attributed to the nuns in the *Therīgāthā* and to the monks in the *Theragāthā*. However, the texts reveal that the Buddha never attempted to create an alternative institution to patriarchal society. Possibly, the Buddha endeavoured for an alternative understanding that could go beyond the patriarchal ethos with his main focus on attaining liberation. Indeed, a comparison between the texts brings to light the practical situations in which the juxtaposition of varied attitudes of androcentrism, patriarchal divisions, misogyny and, at other times, attitudes devoid of gender bias prevailed. One cannot be oblivious of the inbuilt differences in the motive of the texts used in this study. Renunciation is not the only mode of life approved in Buddhism, nor was married life universally condemned. However, this may only be justified when the *Therīgāthā* and the *Theragāthā* are taken into account. The message espoused by the Jātakas is not renunciation leading to *nibbana*, but *samsara* (worldly life) and how to live a good ethical life in this world. It was addressed to the lay followers of Buddhism in particular. In this chapter this argument will be developed by examining two different aspects of the representation of marriage.

Consent and Conflict

Marriage arranged between families based on certain expected standards was as common as lovers eloping and marrying by choice. There are instances where the dictatorial voice of the patriarch in decision-making becomes apparent. Nonetheless, narratives suggesting the choosing of the groom by the bride or vice versa were not rare. How far individual choice could be executed and beyond what it was limited to can be gauged through the following narratives.

The early Buddhist texts represented marriage as the social institution in relation to which gendered negotiations and contestations were manifested in complex engagements. These negotiations include instances of conflict as well as consent. Gender, class and caste (in that order) were three categories of social distinction which remained important and were found to have impacted attitudes in the wider society as reflected in Buddhist textual representations. This pattern seems to have also been endorsed by the texts.

The Role of the Father in Negotiating Marriages

Instances suggestive of the father of the bride as the main decision-maker in choosing the groom for his daughter are widespread. In one story of the Jātakas,[2] a Bodhisatta was born into a treasurer's family and was known as Cullaseṭṭhi.[3] Once on his way he saw a dead mouse on the road and predicted that any decent young man might start a business by picking this mouse and end up keeping a wife. Overhearing him, a young man of a 'good' family but reduced circumstances, *duggatakulaputto*[4] (poor or reduced to a wretched condition) picked up the dead mouse and sold it to a person who was searching for food for his cat. With that little money he bought some molasses and collected some water in the forest. There he fed the tired flower-gatherers with it. They provided him with flowers which he sold and earned eight coins. Gradually his income increased. By clearing the king's garden and selling the wood he received sixteen coins. As the story progressed we learn that he developed connections with sea and land traders. Then he made new plans and availed opportunities to expand his trade. At the end of the story, the young man went to convey his gratitude to Cullaseṭṭhi and told him how he became so wealthy. On hearing his story, Cullaseṭṭhi felt that such an intelligent young fellow shouldn't fall into the hands of someone unscrupulous. So, he married him to his grown-up daughter and bequeathed to him all the family estates. On his death the young man became the treasurer of the city.

In this narrative we hear the rags-to-riches story of a young man who acted as per the idea of Cullaseṭṭhi and accumulated a large amount of wealth. The treasurer was very impressed on hearing the story of the young fellow who actually benefited from the hint given by him. He at once decided to arrange his daughter's marriage with this young fellow. Here, the passive presence of the treasurer's daughter is noteworthy. She had neither a voice in selecting her groom nor could she have a share in her father's property. She could only be the ground for the exchange of territorial rights of her patriarchal lords. There are certain grounds of negotiations in the narrative that demand attention. The young man because of his ready wit became rich. His qualities could hardly go unnoticed by the rich treasurer who immediately arranged a marriage with his daughter. It remained a tacit understanding in the story that the daughter of a rich person was a coveted prize for any talented man her father selects. It is also noteworthy that the young man did not have any choice in selecting his partner. It was the father of the bride who had the sole right to give his daughter's hand as a prize to the person he considered suitable. Besides, what is notable is the fact that status rested on the individual's relation to the means of production. Despite hailing from a poor family, the young man's initiative and intelligence allowed him access to wealth through a series of trade relations. It was through this change in status that he was married to an affluent household. This strongly speaks in favour of matrimonial relations between equal but not inherited status.

There are some indications of special qualities in a person—like avoiding violence—which are considered important factors for being a suitable groom. This becomes evident[5] through the story of a prince named Dīghāyukumāro[6] who couldn't take revenge for his parents' murder. The prince told the king who killed his parents that he would not harm the king, as revenge breeds hatred—'*Na hi verena verāni sammantīdha kudācanaṁ averena ca sammanti, esa dhammo sanantano ti*.'[7] On hearing this, the king was impressed and gave his daughter in marriage to him and established him in the kingdom that belonged to his father. This was indeed a marriage between individuals of equal status but the prince's non-violent nature is emphasized here. This narrative once again attests to the passive presence of the princess in the entire marriage negotiation.

Turning to the *Theragāthā*, we see that unlike the Jātakas, which focus on qualities of resourcefulness or kindness, the bodily charm of the *thera* becomes an important factor in negotiating marriage. This is evident in the instance of the *thera* Eraka.[8] He was the son of an eminent person. He was charming was successful in everything he did. He was wedded to a maiden suitable in 'beauty, virtue, years and accomplishments'[9] for him. But he was always in search of the Master (that is, the Buddha). Later, the Master gave him certain exercises but his mind was overpowered by evil thoughts and he was admonished by the Master. He realized the futility of worldly attachments and devoted himself to gaining insight. He confessed to the Master that worldly wishes were full of woes and that desire bred suffering. Thus, he repeated the Master's words in his verse, '*Dukkhā kāmā Eraka na sukhā kāmā Eraka, yo kāme kāmayati dukkhaṃ so kāmayati Eraka, yo kāme na kāmayati dukkhaṃ so na kāmayati Erakā'ti.*'[10]

Here, the past life of the renouncer reflects the Buddhist conformism to brāhmaṇical convention (i.e. the *thera* being an affluent householder married to a charming woman) and the devising of a different resolution through the Buddhist doctrine. Notably, here the bride's virtue was a significant marker in the matrimonial alliance. Besides, the physical traits of the groom also had some importance in the narrative.

A close parallel features in the *Therīgāthā* where physical charm has been regarded as a significant factor in a prospective bride. *Therī* Anopamā[11] was born to a treasurer's family and known for her unsurpassed beauty. Her hand was asked for by kings and nobles from different regions; suitors offered rich gifts to her father in exchange for her hand.[12] However, she found no interest in worldly life and chose to join the Order. She asked for the permission of the Buddha to enter the Order and was taught the dhamma.[13]

The narrative emphasizes the physical charm of Anopamā in order to demonstrate the impermanence of physical beauty. Thus, the everyday understanding of conventional female beauty as the main factor in marriages and sensuous desires is undermined. However, Anopamā had the choice to turn away from worldly bargaining and seek bliss in the saṇgha. This perhaps indicates the saṇgha as not entirely organized in terms of patriarchal norms.

There is one shocking narrative where the virginity of the bride was an important concern. This falls under the purview of the representational history of gender in the specific context of early Buddhist conceptions, and the basis for such social information or representation needs to be investigated. This is clear in a story where we hear about a *paṇṇika* (fruit seller).[14] He had a very beautiful and virtuous daughter who was always laughing. A family of similar station asked for her hand in marriage. Her father noticed that she was always laughing loudly, which was not considered a desirable quality in a maiden from a good family. This made her unwanted in the eyes of society and left her parents in disgrace. Hence, her father decided to test her virginity. In order to test his daughter's virtue, he attempted to make love to her. The maiden burst into tears and began to cry out that such a thing would be monstrous. Then the man revealed that his only intention was to know whether his daughter was virtuous. The maiden declared that she never looked on any man with 'eyes of love'[15]—'*Āma tāta atthi, mayā hi lobhavasena nakoci puriso olokitapubbo*'.[16] The father calmed her down, took her back home and gave her away in marriage. Later, he visited the Buddha and described the incident to him. Ironically, the Buddha did not question the immorality of the father's gesture. Instead, a patriarchal value system was seen to be agreed to by the Buddha. This was the same society that he otherwise challenged in many aspects. Here, the sexuality of the maiden is policed to ensure the purity and continuation of prestige of the family in negotiating marriage. The dependence of the family prestige on the sexuality of the maiden becomes clear through the test devised by her father. He brought his daughter back home after being verbally assured of her purity. The tone of the text conforms to the notion of virginity as an essential prerequisite in a bride. Not only did the father of the bride play a significant role in selecting the groom but he was also obsessed with the conventional attributes required of a bride, so much so that he would not stop in testing the virginity of his daughter. What remains surprising is the Buddhist conformism to the patriarchal ethos to the extent that a father could attempt to rape his daughter. This gendered notion of sexuality handed down through myriads of retellings opens to us the scope of further investigation.

The narrative of *therī* Cāpā is also noteworthy.[17] She was born to a family of animal trappers. One day she was asked by her father to take care of an ascetic named Upaka while he was away. Incidentally, the ascetic was mesmerized by her great beauty and desired her. On returning home, Cāpā's father heard of the ascetic's plight. He brought the ascetic to his home and gave his daughter in marriage to him. As the story progressed, Cāpā gave birth to a son. Throughout her marriage she always mocked her husband about his past. For example, whenever her baby cried, Cāpā would sing to him, 'Upakas's boy, ascetic's boy, game dealer's boy, don't cry, don't cry!', essentially mocking her husband about his inclination towards the ascetic life. The narrative also mentioned that whenever he was vexed she would tease him even more. To this, but on hearing her husband said he had a protector and would go to him this he was mocked by his wife even more. Finally, he left home and joined the Buddhist Order. With the passage of time, Cāpā began to miss her husband and became distressed. Through her verse she lamented the absence of her husband. Later, she gave her son to her father and attained arhantship (an arhant is one who has attained nirvana and can show others the path of liberation).[18] In the narrative a different kind of negotiation can be seen. The patriarchal control of the matrimonial alliance has been juxtaposed with the misconduct of the wife. However, she is seen regretting her mistake and following her husband in renouncing worldly ties.

In yet another story, a typical instance of confrontation and negotiation has been represented. Daughters as the ground of contestation for their patriarchal lords is evident.[19] We know of the confrontation between the kings of Kaliṅga and Assaka. The king of Kaliṅga was very strong and had an efficient army. He wanted to wage war but couldn't find a befitting competitor. Being advised by his ministers he decided to send his four beautiful daughters adorned with valuable jewellery in a carriage to travel through every kingdom. The king of Kaliṅga would then declare war on any king who would dare to take them to his harem. The king of Assaka, on the advice of his minister Nandisena, invited the royal maidens to his kingdom. On hearing the news, the king of Kaliṅga declared war on Assaka and was completely routed in the war by the king of Assaka and his people. Moreover, Nandisena asked the defeated king of Kaliṅga to offer a portion of his territory as dowry for his four daughters who were then raised to the position of chief queens by the king of Assaka. The confrontation and negotiation visible in the narrative is interesting. While the confrontation took place between the kings, the negotiation occurred in the form of marriage where the four ladies were won by their husband as war booty from their father. The gender relations in marriage portrayed in the above narrative is significant. The passive presence of the brides stand sharply in contrast to the belligerent patriarchs. Women were objectified as war booty to be exchanged between warmongers. This narrative once again emphasized a matrimonial alliance between individuals of equal status.

Besides the occasional glimpse of a liberal attitude in Buddhist texts, there are simultaneous instances of severe patriarchal control where extreme instances of scaffolding rights by patriarchal lords can be seen. Yet, the strict structure of this patriarchal setup is shaky; its borders are porous and vulnerable as is evident from the following narrative. Consider for example the story of King Mahākaṃsa who ruled the Uttarāpatha.[20] He had two sons, Kaṃsa and Upakaṃsa, and a daughter named Devagabbhā.[21] On the birth of his daughter it was predicted that a son would be born to her who would destroy the lineage of Kaṃsa. The king was so fond of his daughter that he couldn't put her to death. When he died, he left the matter to be settled by his sons. Kaṃsa became king and decided to keep his sister husbandless. He kept her in a watchtower where she was unable to meet anybody. Apart from a servant named Nandagopā and her husband who served the royal maiden, nobody was allowed to visit her. One day, King Upasāgara, on hearing the story of Devagabbhā, fell in love with her. The princess saw him from her tower when he went to meet King Kaṃsa, and she developed feelings for him as well. Upasāgara managed to get inside the tower and meet his beloved by bribing Nandagopā. Later, they got married and she gave birth to a son. It was with the assistance of Nandagopā that her child escaped death. Thus, the above narrative suggests an attempt to police the sexuality of a woman as it posed a threat to her brothers. The father died leaving the matter unsettled. He was affectionate towards his only daughter and avoided any confrontation. However, her brothers confined her to a tower and prevented her marriage from taking place.

The transgression took place through a porous boundary and the woman married her lover. The negotiation between the royal maid and the princess is notable. The maid was instrumental in enabling the princess to escape the patriarchal policing imposed on her. The story begins by positioning the princess in a disadvantageous position. We can see her marginalized experience in her father's mansion. It was the royal servant who played the role of her saviour, and her beloved risked all kinds of perils to free her from her brother's confinement.

In this particular section there is an intriguing juxtaposition of doting fathers and objectified daughters as mere movable objects of their patriarchs. Fathers can be seen playing an important role in arranging the marriages of their daughters. They were often obsessed with the conventional qualities required of a perfect bride. Not only is the passive presence of the daughters glaring; the absence of their mothers in the negotiation is noticeable. What is also significant is that this preoccupation with patriarchy is common to the king and the commoner, cutting across class differences.

The Role of Mothers in Negotiating Marriages

The prominence of the mother in arranging the marriage of her son becomes apparent in the following paragraphs.[22] In continuation with the arguments in the preceding sections, I have tried to bring forth a few issues with regard to the arrangement of matrimonial alliances as represented in the three Buddhist texts, paying attention to the nuances in the narratives. The role of the mother in the matrimonial alliances of her children is quite contrasting. Mothers hardly feature in the case of a daughter's marriage; the father, as a patriarchal lord, dictates the details of such an alliance. However, in the case of a son, the mother plays a leading role in determining the entire course of the marriage. I have provided multiple examples of this and explained their different contexts below to elaborate on my argument.

Once, a Bodhisatta was born into a poor family. His father died young and the son supported his widowed mother. He was married forcibly on her request. After the passage of a few days he asked his wife to earn her living as he wanted to renounce the world. His wife told him that she was pregnant and asked him to stay back till she gave birth. Later, the man realized that gradually he was getting involved in the chains of family life. He immediately decided to break the shackles of worldly life and renounce everything. From this we can see that besides evidences indicating patriarchal supervision in the wedding of daughters, the mother often surfaces as the decision-maker in the marriage of her son. In opposition to the marriage of daughters, certain leniencies were visible in the role of mothers in arranging their sons' marriages. This is because Buddhism was more inclined towards encouraging men to overcome worldly ties and join the saṇgha. This was not the case for women as they had a different socio-economic value in contemporary society. Thus, the Buddhist texts were not very particular about the marriage of sons, like they were about daughters, assigning some freedom to women (i.e. mothers) in this context.

A mother becoming desperate to get her son married can be seen in the instance of *thera* Samudda.[23] The *thera* was born to a wealthy councillor and at his prime left the world for the Order. His mother was sad seeing others' sons enjoying married life with their family. Seeing her in such a pensive state, a courtesan offered to entice her son. Samudda's mother immediately promised that if she was able to get married to her son and bring him back from the Order, she would make her the mistress of the family. However, all of the courtesan's attempts ended in vain. *Thera* Samudda uttered his *gāthā* (canonical verse) and described his experience of taming his mind against Māra's evil power. He exclaimed, 'Seeing that public woman making plea, and proffering obeisance gaily decked, in brave array like snare of Mara laid, thereat arose in me the deeper view: attention to the fact and to the cause. The misery of it all was manifest; distaste, indifference the mind possessed; and so my heart was set at liberty . . . .'[24]

A mother being adamant for her son to lead a married life is apparent in the instance of *thera* Ātuma as well.[25] His mother proposed to find him a wife during his adolescence. Soon after, he realized the futility of domesticity and left the world to join the Order. However, his mother was resolute enough to follow him there and 'corrupt' his pious ways. In his *gāthā*, he explained to his mother how marriage is a hindrance in his noble way to wisdom as well as the impossibility of changing his decision in attaining arhantship.[26]

While comparing the above two instances of either of the parents taking the initiative in arranging the marriage of their children, a few issues become apparent. Often, the father could be seen as the sole decision-maker in selecting a befitting groom for his daughter. Mothers do not seem to have a role in this. In contrast, mothers could be seen playing a role in negotiating the marriage of their sons. However, the relative success of fathers becomes apparent in arranging the marriage of their daughters. This stood in sharp contrast to that of the initiative of mothers which often ended in failures. Often they could be seen requesting or persuading their sons with the prospect of a good match. This attitude is absent in the case of the fathers who were regarded as the ultimate authority for their daughters. This might be indicative of a more flexible situation for men in choosing a life of a householder or become an ascetic. It is also significant that fathers are rarely shown as controlling or deciding the marriage of their sons (which, as mentioned earlier, was left to the mothers). In other words they are not as preoccupied with patriliny as the brāhmaṇical texts suggest.

Both Parents Playing an Equal Role in Arranging Marriage

In some instances the consent of both the parents is also mentioned. The instances where both parents played an important role in negotiating their son's marriage were not rare. This surfaces clearly in the story where we come to know of a Bodhisatta who was born into a brāhmaṇa's family and studied at Takkasilā.[27] His parents wanted him to get married but he had no desire for a married life and wanted to embrace the life of an ascetic. When repeatedly urged by his parents, he made a golden image of a maiden and told them 'If you can find me a maiden like unto this, I will take her to wife.'[28] In the village of Kāsi, a maiden named Sammilllabhāsinī matched the perfection of the golden image made by the Bodhisatta and was married to him. We come to know from the story that she was 'endued with all the marks of female beauty'.[29] The above narrative progresses with the Bodhisatta confronting his parents. He wanted to embrace asceticism and had no interest in marriage. His position of rigidity was compromised as a maiden matching all the standards set by him was found; thus, he had to marry her. However, his wife wanted to become his partner and renounce the worldly life. In this story, the negotiation on the part of the wife can be seen. She had to suit all the standards set by the Bodhisatta to become his wife. The lack of any reciprocation on the part of the Bodhisatta reveals the inequal positions between the two in the marriage.

Occasionally, love marriages conducted with the consent of parents were observed in the Buddhist texts.[30] It was predicted that daughter of the king of Madda would live as an ascetic but her son would be a universal monarch. All the kings in the country, hearing this rumour, came together with one accord and surrounded the city. The king of Madda thought if he gave his daughter to one king, the rest of the kings would be enraged. He immediately thought of protecting his daughter. So he fled into the forest with his wife and daughter. There lived in the forest at some distance from his hut the prince of Kaliṅga, who lived there as an ascetic. The king and queen of Madda went to collect food, leaving their daughter in their hut. Incidentally, she met the prince of Kaliṅga on the bank of the Ganges and fell in love with each other. The princess told her parents about the prince and they consented in giving her hand in marriage to him. With the passage of time a son was born to them. He was sent to Kaliṅga, the erstwhile kingdom of his father which the latter had left before coming to the forest. The young prince was made the supreme monarch with celebration. At the end of the story we learn that he took his parents along with him to his kingdom. The fear of the king of Madda that all the kings would be enraged if he arranged his daughter's marriage with any one of them surfaces in the narrative. A resolution was sought in fleeing to the forest. However, the daughter fell in love with an ascetic there. Later, this led the father to accept his daughter's choice and arrange her marriage with him.

Contestation around marriages features in more than one way. Marriages between siblings were not rare. This becomes evident in marriages conducted without the consent of the bride and groom. In the story of the past of the *Udaya Jātaka*,[31] we come to know about the son and daughter born to the king of Kāsi after his queens offered prayers for a son. A son was conceived in the womb of his chief queen and a daughter was born to one of his other wives. They were named Udayabhadda and Udayabhaddā, respectively. As they grew up they were married to each other much against their will. In the course of time the king died and his son ruled the realm. After his death, his wife Udayabhaddā's commands were promulgated, and the courtiers administered the kingdom. Udayabhadda, on his death, became Sakka (another name for the Buddha) in heaven and decided to test Udayabhaddā with wealth and riches. He went inside the seven-storeyed palace with a dish full of golden coins. In the palace Udayabhaddā sat alone, meditating on her virtue. Sakka told her that he was a goblin and asked her to take the golden coins from him. The lady turned down his request immediately and told him that she would not accept anything from any man after her husband's death. Sakka took his leave on hearing this but appeared on the next day but still couldn't make her accept the coins from him. As the story progresses, we learn that as Udayabhadda's identity was disclosed to his wife and she burst into tears. Sakka went back to his heavenly abode after delivering the discourse to her. The very next day Udayabhaddā entrusted her courtiers with the government and herself became a recluse. At the end of the story we come to know that she was born in heaven as Sakka's handmaiden.

From these examples it becomes evident that it is difficult to define the compromises and contestations regarding marriage from a monolithic perspective. We come across a range of evidences hinting at such differences. Instead of having norms dictated by the normative texts, we notice a juxtaposing of varied attitudes in the Jātakas. Contrary to the previous narrative where a lady married an ascetic and brought him to the householder's life, here the lady renounced worldly life and became a recluse. The diverse possibilities regarding renunciation are indicative of the flexibility and fluidity in the Jātakas which stand sharply contrasted to the *Therīgāthā* and the *Theragāthā*.

Another similar example is of *therī* Sumedhā[32] who took an independent decision to renounce the world. On hearing the decision of her parents and kinsfolk regarding arranging her marriage, she clearly told them that her duty did not lie in the household. Her parents were unable to dissuade her of her decision to join the Order. She cut her hair and emphasized the impermanence of temporal existence. Thus, she broke the worldly ties and embraced a life of asceticism. In her verse we can discern her attitude beyond the typical patriarchal setup. The verse initially hints at the conventional mechanism of arranging marriages by parents and kinsfolk. However, the instance of her eloquent voice in rejecting the entire negotiation of marriage is rare in these works. She told her relatives about her understanding of the meaning of life and emphasized the meaninglessness of existence.[33] Sumedha told her mother that most people could not understand the truths taught by the Buddha and hence suffer. To convince the prospective groom about her disdain for worldly pleasure she cut off her hair and threw it on the floor.

Instances of peaceful married life were rare but not uncommon in Buddhist texts. A story from the *Suci Jātaka* hints at the peaceful wedded life of a blacksmith who married his master's daughter.[34] There were both of equal status and the match was approved by both families. The blacksmith won the love of his wife by impressing her father with his craft. However, the turning point in such a marriage in seen in the instance of the *therī* Sujātā,[35] who chose a life of asceticism over a happily married life. Her marriage was arranged by her parents with a person of equal rank. She had a happy married life with him. One day while returning with her attendants, she saw the Master and her heart was drawn towards him.

As the narrative progresses we come to know that she renounced the world and attained arhantship. The occasional mention of a happy married life hints at the influence of lay supporters over the composition of *gāthās*. However, the mention of asceticism as a better option even to a happy married life shows a strong inclination towards the Buddhist ethos.

However, in the instance of the *thera* Vīra[36] a parallel situation of renunciation crops up with notable differences. Vīra was reborn into the family of a minister of King Pasenadi. The constant emphasis on the suitability of his name as per his well-built physical stature is evident in the text. As the commentary progresses, it becomes apparent that he got married according to his parent's choice. Later on, a son was born to him and at that very moment he realized the futility of worldly existence and decided to renounce his worldly life. As he began a life of an arhant his former wife made attempts to lure him back to his family; however, she failed. Here, his name 'Vīra' signified the strength of his mind. He told that it would be as impossible to lure him as shaking a mountain. 'Victor is Vira, free from creeping dread; his is the goal supreme and steadfast strength.'[37] His wife, hearing the same, was extremely influenced and deeply moved. She herself realized the futility of domestic life and joined the order.

While narratives of men and women opting out of marriage figure in the *Theragāthā* and the *Therīgāthā*, women renouncing the world are conspicuous by their absence in the Jātakas. These narratives only acknowledge the male renouncer.

Choosing and Rejecting Partners

Apart from the stories suggesting the negotiation of marriages by parents, we also come across narratives describing eloping couples. There are some instances of women planning to elope with the men they loved. For example, there is story of a Bodhisatta who was born in a brāhmaṇa household.[38] His wife died at an early age leaving him with a son. The Bodhisatta adopted a religious life and went to live in the Himalayas with his son. One day, in the absence of the Bodhisatta, a damsel appeared in their hermitage and asked his son to elope. His son waited till his father returned and decided not to go with the woman. This story clearly hinted at the intrinsic seductive nature of women. Although it becomes clear that eloping was not rare in society, the damsel in the narrative failed to overpower the brāhmaṇa's son. Instead of taking his own decision, he waited for his father's consent.

Instances of eloping with a person of 'lower' social status are also observed in the Buddhist texts.[39] The daughter of a rich merchant in Rājagṛha stooped to intimacy with a slave. Aware of the consequences, she decided to abscond with him stealthily with her belongings. They started living together in a faraway place. It was after she conceived that she realized the necessity of being with her parents at the time of delivery. Her husband, conscious of his great offence, dared not return. The wife, realizing his dilemma, decided to go alone to her parent's place to deliver her baby. Her husband, returning home, realized that his wife had set off for her journey without telling him. He immediately ran after her and came up to her on the road. There she was in labour and ultimately gave birth to a son who was named 'Mahāpanthaka'[40] as he was born on the road. Later, his brother was born in an identical way and came to be known as 'Cullapanthaka'.[41] As they grew up they realized they didn't have any relatives or grandparents, unlike their friends. Due to their constant plaguing, their mother decided to take them to their grandparent's mansion at Rājagṛha.

The rich merchant on hearing of his daughter's return expressed his grief but refused to meet her. He stated that such an offence by one's own children could not be forgiven. He sent a sum of money and asked his daughter to leave but said that she could send her sons to his mansion, if she wished. The daughter took the money and left her sons with her parents.

This narrative hints at the socio-economic significance symbolized by a marriage. Here, the rich merchant was very affectionate towards his daughter. Yet he couldn't accept her marriage to a slave. The daughter was disowned by her parents because of her 'mistake' of marrying a man of relatively 'low' status. She attempted to go to her parents both times she was pregnant but returned without meeting them. Her husband's reluctance to face her parents is apparent. The partial acceptance of the marriage by her parents can be seen in their sending money for her and in the rearing of her children in their custody. Possibly, the children of such marriages were accepted in society but the marriages were still considered a transgression.

The juxtaposition of liberal attitudes and social pressures were not rare in the verses of *therīs*. In the narrative of the *therī* Abhirūpa Nandā,[42] we come to know about her rebirths. She was a lady of peerless beauty and born to the chief wife of a Sākiyan. As the narrative progressed, we see that on the day she was to choose among her suitors, her young Sākiyan kinsman died. What followed is interesting: her parents forced her to renounce the world and join the Order. In the saṇgha, she remained infatuated with her beauty. Fearing the Master's rebuke she avoided meeting him. One day she was compelled to meet him. The Master explained the impermanence of the bodily charm that she took pride in. It was only after this realization that she could attain arhantship.

In the above narrative we come across several social attitudes. An event was held in the town where *therī* Abhirūpa Nandā had the liberty to choose her husband. Paradoxically, the death of her kinsman on that particular day deprived Nandā of the right to be a part of the temporal world. Perhaps the social pressure on her parents was so great that they forced her to join the Order. This hints at the fact that ostracizing the woman for such reasons was common. Yet they had a viable alternative to their worldly life in the saṇgha.

Rejecting proposals of cohabitation by ascetics was rare but not impossible as is evident from the following story.[43] A Bodhisatta was born as a brāhmaṇa's son in the village of Kāsi. He attained perfection in studies and embraced the religious life. He lived by a natural lake, cultivating Attaintments. After wrestling all night long in the spirit, in the morning he bathed and let his body dry. At that moment a daughter of the gods observed his perfect beauty and fell in love with him. She tried to tempt the Bodhisatta by saying that this was the perfect time for enjoying pleasure and he could lead a life of asceticism during the later days of his life. The Bodhisatta rejected her proposal and the nymph vanished at once. Here, the advance made by the nymph in choosing her partner was nullified by the strong-willed ascetic.

It would also be interesting to examine the instances of unmarried women and the social attitudes towards them. In the narrative of the *therī* Selā,[44] we come to know that her meritorious births led to her birth in the royal family. She came to be known as 'the Ālavīkan'[45] as she was born in the kingdom of Ālavi. As the story went one, we learn that her father, the king, was ordained by the Master. Selā, who was unmarried at the time, accompanied her father to hear the Master preach. As time passed, she joined the Order and attained the status of an arhant. It was Māra who stood as a hindrance in her way of attaining *nibbāna* and asked her to choose the sensuous path. Only with her knowledge could she overcome all the hindrances that stood in her way.

This narrative depicts how the princess came to be identified by the name of her kingdom, Ālavī. She was unmarried and had every liberty to choose the life of joining the Order. Yet we see how Māra, the evil God, stood as a hindrance in her path. The same Māra was not visible in the case of her father, whom she followed in joining the Order. However, with her knowledge she eventually overcame Māra. This particular narrative juxtaposes several perspectives of Buddhist religious traditions in conforming to the prevailing gender conventions of society. Here we come across *therī* Selā who had an independent mind and a reputable social identity due to her meritorious birth. She was one of those privileged women who was allowed to listen to the Buddha. She nurtured the desire to renounce the world. Yet, renunciation was not a smooth path as she had to overcome many hurdles in the form of Māra who stood in her way. This represents the inner conflict of Ālavīkan with her strong desire to renounce and the conventional norms she grew up with. Her implicit conformation to the norms of society stood in her path, even if she did follow them subconsciously. She realized these norms to be a form of Māra when she tried to break the shackles of worldly life and embrace liberation. Thus, she realized she was chained only after she tried to move. This verse brings forth multiple Buddhist perspective towards renunciation. First, being a woman of high status, Selā had certain privileges and was able to directly access to Buddhist discourse. Second, she later developed a desire to achieve *nibbāna* and renounce all her comforts and riches. Yet, the gender bias ingrained in

Buddhist ethos surfaces in the representations. She could join the Order but not without having to face a multitude of hurdles. Based on this, I propose that the Buddha had no intention of challenging all the social inequalities in contemporary society, but tried to show people alternative possibilities to conventional societal norms.

The circumstances become intriguing when *gāthās* depict *theras* combating certain complex situations. In the instance of *thera* Posiya[46] there is a repetition of the former commentaries where the *theras* were seen severing their domestic ties after childbirth. However, in this commentary we see that the *thera* went to his home after achieving arhantship. His former wife was unaware of his disposition and tried to attract him towards her but he silently left for the forest. This narrative had a clear hint of the strength of character of the *thera* whereby he could stand by the choice he made.

In the case of *thera* Nandaka,[47] who after hearing the Master teach attained arhantship, he was ranked foremost among all his brothers and sisters in the brethren. One day he went to collect alms in Sāvatthī and met his former wife. She tried to lure him with a seductive smile but in vain. In his *gāthā* the *thera* explained the futility of bodily pleasure, emphasizing its temporality.

Another example occurs in the case of *thera* Uttiya, which closely parallels a narrative in the Jātakas.[48] After entering the Order, he visited his village for a day. On the way, he was mesmerized by the singing voice of a woman. Immediately he was overpowered by acute passion. However, he checked himself by the power of insight. In his *gāthā* he depicted the entire experience of liberation from worldly distractions—'Sound of sweet voice bewildering self control, If one but think upon the image dear, the heart inflamed in feeling doth o'erflow and clinging stayeth. Thus in him do grow the deadly taints bring Saṇsāra near.'[49]

Embedded disturbances in the path of religion become evident in varied ways. In the instance of *thera* Sāṭimattiya,[50] he was born to a brāhmaṇa's family and entered the Order. He soon became a preacher and instructed many *bhikkhus*. He was invited by a family whom he converted to the path of religion. There he was provided food and taken care of by the only daughter of the family. One day Māra, the evil spirit, thought of disturbing the serenity of the *thera* and disgracing him. He took the form of *thera* Sāṭimattiya and touched the maiden. The maiden recoiled, sensing that to be no human touch. However, others in the family saw the incident and lost faith in the *thera*. Later, the *thera* Sāṭimattiya made them aware of the reality of the situation and the master of the house begged his forgiveness.

Along with the examples of wives ensnaring husbands-turned-ascetics, Buddhist texts hint at the courtesan as symbolic of charm and worldly snares for men. Though not bound by nuptial ties, her bodily charm was enough to derail men. Often in the descriptions of the *theras*' past lives, we see them squandering wealth and becoming paupers because of expensive courtesans. This is seen in the case of *thera* Rājadatta[51] who was born to a rich household and squandered wealth on a beautiful courtesan. At one point he became penniless and had to starve. Wandering about, he came to a place where the Master was teaching the norm to his followers. On hearing him Rājadatta understood the temporality of worldly existence and entered the Order. Incidentally, another merchant like him spent money on the same courtesan and lost his wealth. The courtesan was caught soon after and was killed brutally. On seeing her corpse Rājadatta realized the temporal state of the human body and thus was confirmed in his insight and gained arhantship.

The difference in attitude towards two women—wives and courtesans—of the worldly existence is noteworthy. The wife often stood as an obstacle in the path of salvation for the husband. Buddhist texts labelled women as lustful, evil and beyond cure. However, in this case the courtesan who was the cause of derailing men was murdered. Possibly, the independent and powerful existence of the courtesan required a brutal end as 'punishment'. I believe this was because her independence and charm posed a strong threat to the monks, who found it difficult to overcome. Thus, it is common to see textual representations being more stringent in dealing with courtesans as opposed to wives (who were considered less immoral in comparison).

Confessions about the evil of the past life are crucial in some *gāthās*. The instance of *thera* Gotama[52] reveals that he was entrapped in evil company in his past life. He was born to a brāhmaṇa's family and had spent all his wealth on a courtesan. Later, after seeing the Master he attained arhantship and entered the Order. On being asked by a lay companion about his wealth, he confessed about his past unchaste life. He emphasized the peace experienced by a man who could ward off the company of women—'*Sukhaṃ supanti munayo ye itthīsu na bajjharesadā ve rakkhitabbāsu yāsu saccaṃ sudullabhaṃ.*'[53]

Locating consent and conflict in the representations of marriage in the early Buddhist textual traditions suggests the following: repeated instances of marriages being arranged as per the decision of parents make us wonder about the individual choice of the couple. Although elopement was visible in the narratives it was not considered a viable alternative. We have seen how the descriptions varied in the three different texts used here.

Yet, the idea of marriage being conducted mostly by parents and kinsmen as ideal was common in all the texts considered here. The instances of transgressions are contained in the text in the acceptance of children born of those marriages by the fuming parents of the woman. Besides the question of an individual's consent in marriage, instances of individuals not marrying at all and seeking liberation were no less a choice made by the individual. However, such representations appear only in the *Therīgāthā* and the *Theragāthā* and for men in the Jātakas. What becomes significant is the frequent reference to evil company and the conflict with the evil spirit Māra, whom *bhikkhus* and *bhikkhunīs* were always advised to shun.

The repeated emphasis on virginity as an important factor for a perfect wife is sharply in contrast to the lack of evidence suggesting the same in a groom. Besides, it is apparent that the emphasis on physical appearance as an important factor for negotiating marriage features more prominently in the Jātaka narratives compared to the *Therīgāthā* and the *Theragāthā* where physical beauty has been repeatedly undermined as impermanent.

There are other interesting features as well. 'Wise' men are ultimately shown as rejecting marriage in both the Jātakas and the *Theragāthā*. Women in the Jātakas, on the other hand, frequently accept or choose marriage. It is only in the *Therīgāthā* that we find examples of women rejecting marriage.

This actually hints at the varied target audiences in the texts. Jātakas were meant for common folk and the content reflected the everyday lives of the masses. There the narratives deal with more mundane issues and examples that would easily convey a Buddhist solution to the common people. Issues like virgin wives and physical charm were more relatable to them. Thus, the narratives used these examples and their contexts to show Buddha's intervention in such issues and a possible 'Buddhist' solution. So, in many instances Buddha follows a balanced approach to find a compromise between conventional social norms and an alternative path that let the people reflect and look withing themselves. However, in the *Therīgāthā* and *Theragāthā* the approach of the text changes. The content hints a different audience. Each of the instances focus more on the obstacles that stood in the way of the monks'/nuns' liberation. Despite several challenges, women in *Therīgāthā* had more agency in deciding the course of their life. This text was meant for that section of the audience who already had Buddhist inclinations, as lay followers.

Representation of Social Status in Negotiating Marriage

Classification in the Buddhist tradition was twofold—high and low. However, status was not considered permanent and was related to the control over the means of production. Difference in status never received divine sanction as represented in the brāhmaṇical texts.[54]

Despite the fact that inherent status was denied in the Buddhist tradition the recognition of endogamy was clearly manifested. The purity of lineage played a crucial role, mainly among the ruling class. At the same time transgressions were not rare. We get hints of *anuloma* and *pratiloma* marriages[55] in several instances. However, since there was no reference for caste as such but only to birth and lineage, the use of the terms '*anuloma*' and '*pratiloma*' might be understood at most as a prototype of the brāhmaṇical tradition. Although this categorization found firm ground in the *Manusmṛti*, its reflection could also be seen in the Buddhist narratives. The question explored pertains to how class difference influences marriages. Not everyone was willing to concede to the unequal social relations of the hegemonic, brāhmaṇical ideology, which were contested and compromised with at various levels. The Buddhist tradition kept alive the critique of caste.[56] In the Buddhist textual traditions the all-pervasive notion of class differences in society is evident. Although endogamous ties were considered ideal, a different picture emerges, which the following examples will establish.

An instance of upward mobility of women by marriage is found,[57] where we learn about a fat and badly dressed country woman, who worked for hire. As she passed near the courtyard of a palace, a pressing natural need came upon her. Bending down with her clothes decently gathered round her, she accomplished her purpose. Incidentally, the king was impressed by the entire thing as he saw her from his palace. He thought that a woman who could manage this with so much decency must enjoy good health and she must be clean in her home. Therefore, a son born to such a clean lady would grow up cleanly and be virtuous. Thus, the king decided to make her his queen consort. Here we see that a decent habit in women has been emphasized as a significant attribute in negotiating marriage. In fact, she achieved the status of the chief queen despite her marked class difference with the king.

One of the most relevant examples has been discussed in the Jātakas.[58] This narrative tells us of the inherent class attitude among the elite in society as graphed by the composers of the *Pāli Jātaka*. Brahmadatta was the king of Banaras; a Bodhisatta was his minister and adviser. The king fell in love with a *paṇṇikadhīta* (daughter of a fruit seller)[59] on hearing her voice and raised her to the rank of the chief queen after marrying her. With the passage of time the maiden, intoxicated with pride and the affluence of royal life, not only became completely oblivious of her life as a jujube seller, but also failed to recognize the jujube fruit which her family traded. The king became wrathful at her pride and said, 'O daughter of a greengrocer, dealer in ripe jujubes, do you not recognize the jujubes, the special fruit of your family?'[60] He said, 'Bare headed and meanly clad, my queen, thou once didst feel no shame, to fill thy lap with the jujube fruit, and now thou dost ask its name; thou art eaten up with pride, my queen, thou findest no pleasure in life, be gone and gather thy jujubes again. Thou shalt be no longer my wife.'[61] As the story progressed we find that the Bodhisatta mediated in the royal couple's quarrel to reconcile them. He said to the king, 'There are sins of a woman, my lord, promoted to high estate: forgive her and cease from thy anger, O king, for it was thou didst make her great.'[62] The king realized his mistake and restored the queen to her former position and they lived together amicably. The above narrative suggests that the king selecting a woman from a relatively 'lower' status was not rare. On the one hand, the lady was elevated to the position of the chief queen by the dint of her qualities. On the other hand, her fragile position is evident when she was demoted from the royal position by the king. This indicates that although royal marriages took place beyond the class barrier, the functioning of the hierarchy was revived during moments of crisis. The narration highlights the elitist attitude of the king of the realm who also happened to be a devout follower of the Buddha. It took him only a moment to demote his chief queen when he found her 'unsuitable'. The story clearly mentions how he insulted her by reminding her of her low origins. The attitude was, in a way, endorsed by the Master himself as the Buddha did not rebuke the king's arrogant and class-conscious attitude. Instead, he blamed the king for making a wrong choice when he should have compromised.

Another outcome resulting from royal marriages conducted with persons of lower status features in another story in the Jātakas.[63] King Brahmadatta of Benaras fell in love with a woman singing in a garden. As they became intimate the lady conceived a Bodhisatta. The king gave her a signet ring from his finger and told her to spend it on nurturing the child if a girl was born to her or to bring the child with the ring to the palace if it was a son. With the passage of time, the Bodhisatta was born to the woman. As he grew up his friends called him 'no father'.[64] He enquired from his mother about his father and came to know that he was the son of a king. Seeing her son determined to meet his father, she took him to the palace with the ring. Out of shame the king pretended not to recognize her. The woman proclaimed that she would prove the truth. Accordingly, she threw her son in the air and he didn't fall to the earth. It is only then that the king accepted him as his son and made the lady his queen-consort. The Bodhisatta became the king of the realm after his father died and ruled righteously. Here, the negotiation between the king and a woman of relatively 'lower' status for desire is evident and the symbolic role of the signet ring is notable. The bargaining between the maiden with the king and, later on, the confrontation regarding the identity of their child is noteworthy. What can be presumed from the situation is the textual attempt to accommodate affairs that took place beyond conventional marriage norms. This narration is not exactly an example representing marriage negotiations but narrates class discrimination in the context of liaisons struck by kings with common maidens. Such examples are pregnant with far-reaching social messages.

This story is a definite prototype of the *Mahābharata* story of Śakuntalā, the historical significance of which has been critically reviewed by Romila Thapar.[65]

To better comprehend the complexity of the inclusive spirit in the Buddhist portrayal of exogamous marriages, we should further consider the instances of union between people of unequal status. Bestowing one's family identity to a child born to a mother of lower origin was not a smooth process. A relationship with a person of relatively 'lower' origin can be seen in the story of a Bodhisatta who was born as a *purohita* in Benaras.[66] He fell in love with a lady in the park and took her to his abode. With the passage of time, a child was born to her out of wedlock. After the child's birth she told the Bodhisatta, that she would like to name the child after his grandfather. The Bodhisatta thought this would be a disgrace to his family honour. While taking her leave he gave her a signet ring and told her that if a son was born to her she could bring him to the priest. He added that she should use the ring for the child's upbringing, in case a daughter was born to her. In this particular narrative the son of a wealthy *purohita* yielded to desire and had intercourse with a woman of 'lower' origin. Yet, he refused to give any recognition to the child born out of the union. He chose that very moment as ideal to remain loyal to his family, and probably realized the possible disgrace such a clandestine union could bring to his lineage. He resorted to a cheap bargain: of bestowing the maiden with a signet ring that she could use for her child (depending, of course, on the gender of the child to be born) as dictated by him. However, the tone of the text is rather neutral about the entire incident as the Bodhisatta happens to be the *purohita*'s son. Even if he could accept a son born out of wedlock in a 'disgraceful' union, a daughter never featured in his choice. This hints at the vulnerable position of women in the gender relations of society and makes us aware of the uncomfortable position of Buddhism regarding the status of women.

A completely different aspect of marriage between people of unequal status crops up where we discover that besides the physical charm and other attributes, donating to a *bhikkhu*'s saṇgha was a desired quality in a prospective bride and could result in her alliance with a family of higher status. It is hardly surprising that the early Buddhists were inclusive of the lay society in many aspects and had a substantial amount of influence on the same. Given the targeted audiences of the Jātakas (i.e. lay followers), it is imperative to valorize alms-giving as an important quality. This is made clear in the story of Queen Mallikā. She was the daughter of the chief garland-maker of Sāvatthī.[67] She possessed great beauty and was known for her many qualities. She attained merit by giving gruel to the Master and bowing before his feet. The Master predicted to his disciple Ānanda that this girl would become the queen of Kosala. As the story progresses, we see how she was made the chief queen of Kosala by the region's king. Hearing her singing the king was attracted by her voice. He then came to learn about her merit. Learning that she was unmarried, he mounted her on his horse and carried her to his kingdom. Here we find the careful considerations of the varied attributes in the daughter of a garland-maker. She had the required qualities of a desired bride and on top of that she achieved immense merit by practising sincere devotion and almsgiving to the Master. Thereupon we could see the Master predicted her future in the royal household as the queen of Kosala. This immediately speaks in favour of marriages taking place beyond the conventional structure of equal status. The practice of giving alms is suggested as the reason for her miraculous fortune and points to the flexibility of the endogamous structure of marriage.

In another story from the Jātakas, marriage conducted between men and women of different origins has been looked down upon.[68] The king of the golden geese paired with a crow at the feeding ground. A son was born to them, who had no resemblance to his parents. He stayed in a far-off place with his mother and the golden goose would often visit him. The golden goose had two other sons, geese like himself. Later, they discovered that their father had a mate in a faraway place and she had given birth to his child. The sons immediately set off to bring their stepbrother home. On the way, the younger bird tried to prove his superiority, oblivious to the fact that his brothers were older and more experienced than him. On returning, the golden goose was informed about the misconduct. He immediately sent him back to his mother. Here we find the resonance of the treatment of unequal unions in the human world.

All the above examples show us the different outcomes of marriages resulting out of alliances with women of 'lower' origin. A hint at their inborn maleficent traits is common almost to all these tales. However, such women could be fantasized about and desired by men of 'higher' birth. Yet, a marriage with her was, in most cases, considered damaging to the family honour. One can see the multiple perspectives of the Buddhist texts in addressing the prototypes of *anuloma* marriages. Marriages did occur beyond the ideal structure but were not unanimously accepted by society. While some stories indicate the Buddha's mediation in perpetuating *anuloma* marriages, there are many other narratives hinting at the dilemma in sanctioning such a marriage until a son was born. However, the *Therīgāthā* and *Theragāthā* are less preoccupied with these complexities. They concentrate much more on the difference between the married state and that of the renouncer.

In addition to the examples reflecting *anuloma* marriages, the practice of *pratiloma* marriages was also not rare. Instances where a man from a relatively 'lower' status could achieve upward social mobility by a matrimonial alliance features in a story from the Jātakas[69] where a Bodhisatta was born in a very poor *kammārakule* (family of a blacksmith).[70] As he grew up, he became excellent in the art of blacksmithing. Near his village there lived a principal smith, who happened to be the king's favourite. The smith's daughter was exceedingly beautiful and had all the auspicious marks of a renowned woman. Hearing about her beauty, the Bodhisatta thought of making her his wife. Their preference for each other was approved and the marriage was arranged by the father of the bride. However, in contrast to the earlier situation where women of 'lower' birth could be wooed, here, the woman was won with the approval of her father and after the groom proved his worth by excelling in his father-in-law's trade. Also, although poor, the man showed the same craft specialization as his father-in-law.

On the contrary, a man being strictly penalized for desiring a lady of 'high' birth features in another Jātaka narrative.[71] A barber visited the Licchavī royal household regularly to do his job. He used to shave and dress the hair of the king, the queen and the princes. One day, he brought his son with him for assistance. Seeing a Licchavī girl dressed up in finery like a nymph, the son set his heart on her. He was so blinded by desire that he became oblivious of the difference in status between them. The barber told his son about the impossibility of his alliance with a 'high-born' Licchavī woman. He consoled him, saying that he would find him someone who would match his status and station in life. The son was obstinate. He said he would not live if he did not marry the one he desired passionately. On the failure of the barber to make his son see reason, his kinsfolk and friends came to pacify him. The barber's son could not be consoled and he pined for the Licchavī girl until he perished. As the story ends, the barber can be seen performing his obsequies and visiting the Master. Here, a man of 'lower' origin realized his mistake at the cost of his life as he desired a woman of 'higher' status. The acknowledgment of the inbuilt division in society between the relatively 'high' born and the 'lowly' has been very clearly manifested. The barber was so aware of his status that he warned his son about the impossibility of such a union. He had shown him the prospect of a better alliance according to his own status. What is noticeable is that the Licchavī lady remains invisible in the entire matter. The barber's son, in spite of passionately desiring her, never conveyed this to her.

In earlier discussions in this chapter, the stories of men of higher birth copulating with women of relatively lower origin survived in different variants, relating to the multilayered complexities of the patriarchal society. However, in a reversed situation in which a woman of high birth is associated with someone from a lower status we do not visualize the same ambiguity. The structure of the narratives where poor or relatively 'low-status' men become a potential hindrance in proposing marriage are more established. This becomes clearer in a story where a jackal fell in love with the lioness.[72] Here, a Bodhisatta was born as a young lion, the brother of the aforementioned lioness. A jackal loved in a nearby cave and conveyed his love to the lion's sister, completely oblivious of his 'low' status in the hierarchy of animals. The lioness, being conscious of her royal status, felt insulted by this audacious move. When her brothers returned from the forest, she told them that the jackal had dared to propose marriage to her. The lions were furious and went to kill the jackal. However, in their rage, they ended up dying violent deaths as they took action without reflecting on the matter. The Bodhisatta, however, listened patiently to his sister's complaint and watched his brothers meet their fatal end. He took measured steps to terrorize the jackal, who after hearing the lion roar, died out of fear.

In the above story we see how animals are conceptualized in human terms. The hierarchical division in the animal world symbolizes the lioness's 'high' birth as she was powerful, whereas the jackal has been categorically associated with a menial group of animals positioned low in the hierarchy of the human world. We also observe how the lioness, being of 'high' birth, rejected the proposal of the jackal, who was considered amongst the most vile of animals in the jungle. She was insulted by the fact that an animal of such a 'low' status could propose to her and decided to commit suicide. At the end of the story we come to know how she provoked her brothers to kill the jackal.

Another thought-provoking story discusses a slave named Kalanduka hiding his identity and absconding with the daughter of a treasurer.[73] He took all pleasures from his wife. The treasurer discovered what Kalanduka had done and sent his trusted parrot to find the slave. After searching for a while, the parrot found the slave enjoying the company of his master's daughter by the river. Intoxicated with a pungent drink, the slave spat on his wife's head. At that moment the parrot reminded the slave of his real identity. The parrot also told him what a heinous act he had committed by spitting on the head of a high-status woman. Recognizing the parrot, the slave was afraid of being exposed and attempted to appease him. However, the parrot understood his tricks and went back to the treasurer, informing him of his findings. The treasurer ordered his men to bring back his slave and returned him to his previous, lowly status. In this narrative the slave was reminded of his real status by the parrot who was the messenger of the treasurer. Though the slave escaped with the merchant's daughter and made her his wife, the difference in their status was so glaring that he failed to practise the 'appropriate' gestures while making love to his wife. The slave had originally hidden his real identity from his wife. Thus, he tried to appease the parrot so that his real identity was not exposed.

In contrast to the *anuloma* marriages, the attitude towards the *pratiloma* marriage is varied. Except for a few references to peaceful unions, in most instances *pratiloma* marriages result in more conflict and penalization in the Buddhist textual traditions. Again, we may note that these discussions are restricted to the Jātakas. They do not figure as important themes in the *Therīgāthā* or the *Theragāthā*. Perhaps the *Therīgāthā* or the *Theragāthā* had a targeted audience different from that of the Jātakas, where messages had to be more inclusive and devoid of caste and class discrimination in any form.

Marriage Between Partners of Equal Status

Matrimonial ties between people of equal status were widely regarded as the ideal form of marriage. On some occasions class differences surfaced as a determining factor in negotiating marriage. The failure of a daughter in choosing an appropriate partner testifies to that, which is evident from the following tale.[74] This particular story not only reflects the norms of the human world but also deflects from it. The king of the golden mallards, Haṁsarāja,[75] had a lovely young daughter. The king was so fond of her that he was willing to grant her any boon she wanted. The daughter asked her father to grant her the boon of choosing a husband for herself. The king, in fulfilment of his promise, gathered all the birds and asked his daughter to choose. She chose a peacock with jewelled shine on his neck. Being overwhelmed at his good luck, the peacock, in defiance of all decency, began to dance and exposed himself. The Haṁsarāja was so shocked by his conduct that he decided to not give his daughter in marriage to the peacock. The king then settled his daughter's marriage with one of his nephews. This narrative portrays the confrontation of a doting father and his daughter in fulfilling the promise he made her. His daughter had the liberty to choose a groom for herself. Nonetheless, we find her making a 'wrong' choice. At the end of the story, her father chooses a young mallard for her as a 'suitable' royal groom. This hints at the fact that the royal maiden was not prudent enough to choose a befitting partner. A few things emerge from this narrative; we sense the hierarchical division of the birds' world as represented in the story. Haṁsarāja was placed in a relatively 'higher' position than the peacock. The 'lower' position of the peacock in the hierarchy has been indicated by its lack of manners. Haṁsarāja's daughter got a chance to choose her partner from among all the birds. However, such an arrangement had to be approved of by her father and her choice was immediately turned down when it was considered in appropriate by her father. Here, the phenomenon of social status played an important role in arranging the marriage in the narrative. It becomes clear that all the prospective male birds in the narrative had the discretion to only join the arrangement of being chosen by the bride. Marriage could only be negotiated if the choice of Haṁsarāja's daughter was approved by him. Thus, we get a glimpse of the hierarchical differences in the human world that may have played a crucial role in negotiating marriages.

The representation of marriage arranged between couples perceived to be equals by their community can be best understood in the complexities that developed in some other tales from the Jātakas.[76] One example narrates the story of a female Jain at Vesālī who was in disputation with a learned Jain male. They proved well-matched for each other as disputants. The Licchavīs present there were impressed by their qualities and thought of arranging their marriage. They thought that such a couple with these qualities would surely beget children of great talent. This assumption proved correct, and the couple bore children with great qualities. These children learned a great deal from their scholarly parents. The daughters were schooled by their parents so that if any lay man refuted their thesis, they would become his wives. They added to this, that if ever a priest refuted them they would take orders from him. As the story progresses, we find that these learned daughters were refuted by the venerable Sāriputta. They narrated their parents' words to him and were ordained to sainthood. In the narrative we see how marriages were arranged by the Licchavīs between two befitting partners of high talent. It has been clearly stated in the story that such unions would lead to the birth of children with supreme qualities resembling the parents. Thus, we see how marriage was strategically arranged. Interestingly, the choice of the bride or groom hardly played any role in negotiating the alliance. It was the community that took the ultimate decision.

Instances are not rare where confrontations regarding marriage between two families of varied religious views took place. We find an instance of this in the story where children of two families of different religious views were united in nuptial ties. The woman hailed from a family that were firm believers in the Buddhist faith while the groom's family practised another heretical religion. The daughter of one family possessed all the supreme qualities of human existence.[77] Being impressed by her qualities another family of equal social rank to her parents asked her hand for their son. Initially her parents turned down the proposal. They said that the family, despite being of equal rank, had heretical views. They dreaded that their daughter would not be allowed to practise almsgiving after her marriage into such a family. As their offer was rejected, the family assured the daughter's parents that she would be permitted to do everything she desired. Eventually, the marriage was celebrated during an auspicious season. The bride performed all her duties faithfully towards her in-laws. With time she succeeded in changing the heretical views of her husband and every person in his family. As the story went on, the young lady, by reason of her own faith, became an ascetic along with her husband.

At the same time, Buddhist traditions allow for certain ambivalent situations. This ambivalence is even more marked in instances where the representation of marriage between people of equal statuses failed.[78] We learn this in the story of the daughter of the servant of the Master's chief disciple. She was married to a person of befitting status but her husband used to enjoy himself elsewhere and took no interest in her. However, she remained oblivious to all the disrespect shown to her. Like an obsessed learner she spent her time listening to religious preaching and successfully reached 'the fruit of the first path'.[79] With time she realized that her husband did not care for her. Thus, she decided to leave her household and embrace a life of asceticism. Here, the idea of a woman overcoming her worldly ties has been largely based on the fact that her husband took no interest in her and was licentious. Besides, we see that his wife became indifferent about his absence and found respite in striving for arhantship.

Turning to the *Therīgāthā* and *Theragāthā*, we mostly come across examples of marriages between individuals of equal status. In the narrative of the daughter of a poor brāhmaṇa,[80] the former was married to a hunchbacked brāhmaṇa. She was eloquent in telling her husband about her inability to continue the worldly life. She persuaded him to consent to her renouncing the world. In the story, we become aware of her initial combat to overcome desire. It was by practising self-control that she attained arhantship.[81]

The story of Dhammadinnā[82] allows us to have an idea of her married life. Dhammadinnā after several births was born into the family of a clansman at Rājagaha and was married to Visākha, an eminent citizen. It is worth mentioning that Dhammadinnā acquired merit in all her previous births. We come to know that Dhammadinnā's husband decided to break all ties to the temporal world and join the Order. On returning home he remained quiet and abstained from touching his wife. On being asked the reason for his indifference, he said he could not take pleasure in worldly life anymore. He asked his wife to lead her life in whichever way she desired: she could choose to stay in his house or take as much wealth as she needed and return to her natal home. Dhammadinnā made her choice; she decided to break ties with the temporal world and embrace the life of a nun. She asked her husband for permission. As the story progressed, we see she went from the city to the village to achieve serenity. After receiving knowledge in dhamma she decided to go to Rājagaha to the Master. What followed her return is noteworthy. Her husband, hearing of her return, became curious about what she had learnt. He came to meet her, with the purpose of testing the knowledge she acquired. She was able to answer all his questions such as how, 'one might cut a lotus stalk with a knife'.[83] The Master applauded her great wisdom and elevated her rank among the Sisters.

The above two instances are related to the hierarchical framework of society. We see in both the instances that marriage takes place between people of the same status. Although both women belonged to two different echelons of society, respectively, the compulsions imposed upon them were somewhat identical.

Here, a number of issues of gender relations become evident. The text reflects the social constraints of gender relations that were widespread in society at the time. For example, it was only when Dhammadinnā asked her husband the reason for his strange behaviour that he thought it worth explaining, whereas Dhammadinnā could be seen asking for his consent before taking the decision to renounce. Besides, her husband could be seen influencing her choice. He offered her the options of staying in his house or taking a part of his wealth and going back to her natal home. It was Dhammadinnā took an independent decision to embrace a life leading to the attainment of arhantship. What then followed was even more interesting. She acquired knowledge to a level that she was able to meet the Master. Her husband then, in spite of breaking all ties of temporal existence, could not miss the chance of meeting her and testing her knowledge. However, the 'soteriological inclusiveness'[84] of the saṇgha is demonstrated when the Master applauded the wisdom of Dhammadinnā and raised her status in the Order.

An almost identical instance could be seen in the case of the *therī* Vāsiṭṭhī.[85] Her marriage was arranged with a person of equal status. They had a happy married life with a son. It was after the demise of their son that grief engulfed them. While the relatives were consoling her husband, the *therī* left the house maddened with grief. Later, she found solace in the words of the Master and joined the Order.

Prospects of marriages between equals can be visualized in the instance of *thera* Uttara.[86] He was born at Rājagaha to a well-off brāhmaṇa family. He was known for his beauty, wisdom and virtue. Hearing of his reputation, a leading minister of Magadha desired a marriage between Uttara and his daughter. Uttara turned down the proposal as he had no interest in worldly existence and later joined the Order. He had to tread on the path of hardships and evil circumstances. But he was told by the Master that these were the consequences of his previous actions. Finally, he realized the evils of rebirths and thus renounced his worldly life.

In another story *thera* Raṭṭhapāla[87] was born to a very affluent family and was married to a suitable wife. Listening to the Master he became inclined towards religion and with great difficulty obtained permission from his parents to join the Order. Later, he got permission to visit his parents' house. There, a few ladies in fine attire asked him for whose sake he renounced the world. They asked him if the celestial nymphs were attractive enough to entice him to come back to the material world. He explained to them the impermanence of human bodily charm through his *gāthā*.

Instances of taking wives from a suitable class becomes evident in the commentary of *thera* Hārita.[88] He was born to wealthy brāhmaṇa parents and was married to a lady of befitting status. He enjoyed his married life and remained enamoured by his wife's physical charm. He was contented realizing that such beauty would take a long time to decay. It was only after she was bitten by a snake and died that Hārita was absolutely crushed by grief. After listening to the Master speak he realized the impermanence of worldly life. Without any hesitation he severed all his domestic ties and renounced the world. What is noteworthy is that while marriages in the Jātakas between partners of equal status tend to be described as 'happy', the *Therīgāthā* and *Theragāthā* are far more critical towards marriage in general, including those amongst men and women of equal status.

Apart from the structural similarity already pointed out in the texts,[89] the portrayal of gender relations in the context of everyday society is worth mentioning. It is evident from the narratives that each of the texts attempts to reach out to a different group of listeners. The Jātakas, through their description of everyday experiences of all sections of society attempted to reach out to a wider audience. The *Therīgāthā* seems to follow almost the same strategy but with certain limitations: it hints at the possibility of renunciation as a viable alternative for women of all sections of society. On the contrary, a different situation can be seen in the *Theragāthā*, which will be discussed in the following paragraphs.

Marriage has been discussed in all three texts. However, each of the texts had differences in terms of the people they catered to; therefore, we find a different treatment and various resolutions to issues related to marriage. For instance, physical attributes are considered an important factor in negotiating marriages in the narratives of all three texts. However, in the *Theragāthā* we learn more about the impermanence of bodily charm. Instances of elopement are portrayed in the narratives of the Jātakas and commentaries of the *Therīgāthā*, but such situations hardly appear in the *Theragāthā*. In the latter, marriages arranged by parents are the only possibility. This is also because the *Theragāthā* focuses on the lives of monks in the saṇgha and marriages are not discussed very often. However, the description of the courtesan as a hindrance to worldly existence appears common to all the three texts.

Similarly, stories in the Jātakas[90] and the *Theragāthā*[91] portray desperate parents finding a bride similar to a statue of a beautiful maiden made by their son. There are also unique representations of animal characters replicating the gendered world of humans in the narratives of the Jātakas. The use of animal characters does not feature in the *Therīgāthā* and the *Theragāthā*. This, once again, speaks in favour of the more popular perspective represented in the Jātakas. Inspite of these inter-textual disparities, we see the hierarchy of status plays a vital role in matrimonial alliances in all the texts. It is only in the *Theragāthā* that marriage between equal statuses was represented as the only possibility.

Apart from all the above-mentioned comparisons, what is worth mentioning are the instances of the *theras*' insight in the *Theragāthā*. The *Theragāthā* presents a conventional portrayal of women as symbolic temptresses and as obstacles in the path of renunciation of the *theras*. What is a significant departure is the fact that instead of castigating women's character in the *gāthās* for these offences we find *theras* reflecting on these instances and braving such obstacles. This once again bolsters the point mentioned earlier that the content of the texts was audience-specific. Therefore, citing examples of terrorizing women with instances of brutal punishment was unnecessary in the *Theragāthā* as it mostly catered to *bhikkhus*, whereas an emphasis on overcoming obstacles through insight was considered more effective.

In the *Therīgāthā* and *Theragāthā* we only come across marriages arranged between equal statuses. That there is complete silence about any other possibilities for marriage opens the ground for a comparative analysis with the Jātakas. There we see the possibilities of *anuloma* and *pratiloma* marriages happening besides alliances between equals. This possibly indicates the multilayered Buddhist attitude towards marriage. However, it appears from all three Buddhist texts that the endogamous relation was considered to be the ideal norm.

In this chapter, two aspects of marriages have been closely studied. We see certain narratives indicating the significant role played by parents in arranging marriages. This presents us with many issues. The passive presence of the daughter and her mother in some narratives stand in sharp contrast to the mothers' desperation for a good match for their sons. Not only so, eloping lovers posed a challenge to the strict vigilance of patriarchal lords. Besides, the mere present of *anuloma* and *pratiloma* marriages juxtaposed against the conventional form denotes the heterogeneous possibilities contained in the institution of marriage beyond rites and rituals. What is interesting is the coexistence of different possibilities within the institution of marriage. Given the relationship of dependence between the Buddhist saṇgha and the laity, the textual portrayals of marriage offer opportunities for identifying with different possibilities instead of imposing a single, monolithic definition.

NOTES

1. John G. Jones, *Tales and Teachings of the Buddha*, New Zealand: Cybereditions Corporation, 2001, p. 66.
2. E.B. Cowell, ed., *The Jātakas*, New Delhi: Munshiram Manoharlal, 2002, *Cullaka Seṭṭhi—Jātaka*, story no. 4. All the references to the Jātakas are from this translation.
3. V. Fausboll, ed., *The Jātakas Together with its Commentaries*, vol. 1, London: Trubner & Co., 1877–96, p. 120.
4. Ibid., p. 120.
5. Cowell, *Dīghitikosala Jātaka*, story no. 371.
6. See Fausboll, *The Jatakas Together with its Commentaries*, vol. 3, p. 211.
7. Ibid., p. 212.
8. Rhys Davids, *Psalms of the Early Buddhists*, London: Pali Text Society and New York: Luzac and Co., 1964, canto 1, part X, commentary XCII, verse 93. All the references are from this translation.
9. Ibid., p. 86.
10. H. Oldenberg and R. Pischel, *The Thera- and Theri-gatha (Stanzas*

Ascribed to Elders of the Buddhist Order of Recluses) (online version), London: Pali Text Society, 1883, verse 93, see http://gretil.sub.uni-goettingen.de/gretil/2_pali/1_tipit/2_sut/5_khudd/theragou.htm, accessed 10 April 2016.

11. Davids, *Psalms of the Early Buddhists*, cantos 6, commentary LIV, verse 151–6.
12. See Charles Hallisey, tr., *Therīgāthā: Poems of the First Buddhist Women*, London: Murty Classical Library of India, 2015, verse 153.
13. Ibid., verse 155.
14. Cowell, *Pannika Jātaka*, story no. 102.
15. Ibid.
16. Fausboll, *The Jatakas Together with its Commentaries*, vol. 102, p. 412.
17. Davids, *Psalms of the Early Buddhists*, canto 13, commentary LXVIII, verse 291–311.
18. See Hallisey, tr., *Therīgāthā*, verse 308–10.
19. Cowell, *Cullakāliṅga Jātaka*, story no. 301.
20. This term is used in many of the Buddhist texts to denote the northern part of Jambudvipa, extending from Anga in the east to Gandhara in the north-west and from the Himalayas to Vindyas.
21. Cowell, *Ghata Jātaka*, story no. 454.
22. Cowell, *Bandhanāgāra Jātaka*, story no. 201.
23. Davids, *Psalms of the Early Buddhists*, canto 7, commentary CCXXIV, verse 459–65. A parallel story is found in the *Jātakas*, story no. 201.
24. Ibid., pp. 229–30.
25. Davids, *Psalms of the Early Buddhists*, canto 1, part VIII, commentary LXXII, verse 72.
26. Oldenberg and Pischel, *The Thera- and Theri-gatha*, see http://gretil.sub.uni-goettingen.de/gretil/2_pali/1_tipit/2_sut/5_khudd/theragou.htm, verse 72.
27. Cowell, *Ananusociya Jātaka*, story no. 328.
28. Ibid.
29. Ibid.
30. Cowell, *Kāliṅga Bodhi Jātaka*, story no. 479.
31. Cowell, *Udaya Jātaka*, story no. 458.
32. Davids, *Psalms of the Early Buddhists*, canto 16, commentary LXXIII, verse 448–522.
33. Oldenberg and Pischel, *The Thera- and Theri-gatha*, see http://gretil.sub.uni-goettingen.de/gretil/2_pali/1_tipit/2_sut/5_khudd/therigou.htm. Also see Hallisey, tr., *Therīgāthā*, verse 468–9.

34. Cowell, *Suci Jātaka*, story no. 387.
35. Davids, *Psalms of the Early Buddhists*, cantos 6, commentary LIII, verse 145–50.
36. Ibid., canto 1, part I, commentary VIII, verse 8.
37. Ibid., p. 14.
38. Cowell, *Arañña Jātaka*, story no. 348.
39. Cowell, *Cullaka Seṭṭhi Jātaka*, story no. 4.
40. See Fausboll, *The Jatakas Together with its Commentaries*, story no. 4.
41. Ibid.
42. Davids, *Psalms of the Early Buddhists*, canto 2, commentary XIX, verse 19–20.
43. Cowell, *Samiddhi Jātaka*, story no. 167.
44. Davids, *Psalms of the Early Buddhists*, canto 3, commentary XXX, verse 54–6.
45. Ibid., p. 43.
46. Ibid., canto 1, part IV, commentary XXXIV, verse 34.
47. Ibid., canto 4, commentary CLXXXIX, verse 279–82.
48. Ibid., canto 1, part X, commentary XCIX, verse 99. There is a parallel story in the *Jātakas*, story no. 306.
49. Ibid., p. 99.
50. Ibid., canto 3, commentary CLXXIX, verse 246–8.
51. Ibid., canto 5, commentary CXCVIII, verse 315–19.
52. Ibid., canto 2, part 1, commentary CXXIX, verse 137–8.
53. Oldenberg and Pischel, *The Thera- and Theri-gatha*, see http://gretil.sub.uni-goettingen.de/gretil/2_pali/1_tipit/2_sut/5_khudd/theragou.htm, verse 281–2, story no. 137.
54. Uma Chakravarti, *Gendering Caste through a Feminist Lens*, Calcutta: Stree, 2006, p. 47.
55. *Anuloma* or hypergamy is where a man from a higher status marries a woman of low status. *Pratiloma* or hypogamy is where a man marries a woman of higher status.
56. Chakravarti, *Gendering Caste through a Feminist Lens*, p. 92.
57. Cowell, *Bāhiya Jātaka*, story no. 108.
58. Cowell, *Sujāta Jātaka*, story no. 306.
59. Fausboll, *The Jatakas Together with its Commentaries*, vol. 3, p. 21.
60. Cowell, *Sujāta Jātaka*, story no. 306, p. 14.
61. Ibid.
62. Ibid., p. 15.
63. Cowell, *Kaṭṭhahāri Jātaka*, story no. 7.

64. Ibid., p. 28.
65. Romila Thapar, *Śakuntalā: Texts, Readings, Histories*, New York: Columbia University Press, 2011.
66. Cowell, *Uddālaka Jātaka*, story no. 487.
67. Cowell, *Kummāsapiṇḍa Jātaka*, story no. 415.
68. Cowell, *Vinīlaka Jātaka*, story no. 160.
69. Cowell, *Sūci Jātaka*, story no. 387.
70. Fausboll, *The Jatakas Together with its Commentaries*, vol. 3, p. 281.
71. Cowell, *Sigāla Jātaka*, story no. 152.
72. Ibid.
73. Cowell, *Kalaṇḍuka-Jātaka*, story no. 127.
74. Cowell, *Nacca Jātaka*, story no. 32.
75. Fausboll, *The Jatakas Together with its Commentaries*, vol. 1, p. 207.
76. Cowell, *Cullakāliṅga Jātaka*, story no. 301.
77. Cowell, *Suvaṇṇamiga Jātaka*, story no. 359.
78. Cowell, *Asitābhū-Jātaka*, story no. 234.
79. Ibid., p. 159. The 'fruits' here indicate the results of different stages of liberation.
80. Davids, *Psalms of the Early Buddhists*, canto I, commentary XI, verse 11.
81. Oldenberg and Pischel, *The Thera- and Theri-gatha*, see http://gretil.sub.uni-goettingen.de/gretil/2_pali/1_tipit/2_sut/5_khudd/therigou.htm.
82. Davids, *Psalms of the Early Buddhists*, canto 1, commentary XII, verse 12.
83. Ibid., p. 17. This line hints at her promptness in answering all the questions.
84. Alan Sponberg, 'Attitudes Toward Women and the Feminine in Early Buddhism', in *Buddhism, Sexuality and Gender*, ed. Jose Ignacio Cabezon, New Delhi: Sri Satguru Publications, 1992, p. 8.
85. Davids, *Psalms of the Early Buddhists*, canto 6, commentary LI, verse 133–8.
86. Ibid., canto 2, part I, commentary CXXI, verse 121–2.
87. Ibid., canto 16, commentary CCLI, verse 769–75.
88. Ibid., canto 1, part III, commentary XXIX, verse 29.
89. Kumkum Roy, *The Power of Gender and the Gender of Power: Explorations in Early Indian History*, New Delhi: Oxford University Press, 2010, p. 18.
90. Story no. 328.

91. Davids, *Psalms of the Early Buddhists*, canto 18, commentary CCLXI, verse 1051–3.

2

The Working of Marriage and 'Beyond'

ANTONIO GRAMSCI'S notion of cultural hegemony gives us an idea of a non-coercive mode of social dominance. Domination can be a twofold mechanism. On one hand it can be realized through the coercive organ of the state and, on the other hand, it can be operated through non-dominant mechanisms, like the moral policing of society.[1] In the Indian context, the hierarchical structure of the society begins with the family, which has a patriarchal structure. Ideology plays an important role for the sustenance of this hierarchical power structure in society.

In the Buddhist texts we do not find any semblance of the normative way of portraying 'right' and 'wrong' marriages. Yet, there exists a unique strategy of defining the 'proper' and 'improper'. The Jātakas do not directly prescribe Buddhist ethics in the narratives. But most of the stories hint at the practical disadvantages of marriage, resolved with the intervention of the Buddha. It becomes clear that the narratives aimed at a particular way of constructing the 'proper' and 'improper' in the psyche of common folk. Concern for a daughter's chastity before marriage, relationships out of wedlock or adultery have been the subject of many tales in the Jātakas. The variations in conjugal behaviour in the stories may indicate that unlike the brāhmaṇical normative texts, the Jātakas did not intend to present coherent rules of conduct for married life for the lay society. It is only in a few instances, which also occur in the Pāli *Nikāya*, that we get narrations of the Buddha directly preaching moral conduct to lay couples, where a glimpse of the Buddhist conception of ideal conjugal conduct is available. This is found to be heavily overlaid with patriarchal attitude. Portrayals of marital union would obviously be differently constructed in the *Theragāthā* and *Therīgāthā*.

However, in the *Therīgāthā* and the *Theragāthā*, we come across the past lives of the *therīs* and the *theras*, respectively. Here, the practical disadvantages about marriage are often indicated. Unlike the Jātakas, in these texts the solutions to problems faced in past lives of the *therīs* and *theras* lie in breaking all ties with one's worldly life and attaining arhantship. From the verses we get an idea of inconsistency at varied levels in the married lives of the *therīs* and *theras*. The issues observed here include questions of infidelity, self-control and seduction—mostly related to the behaviour of women.

Perceptions Pertaining to the 'Proper' in Marriage

The Buddhist view of the 'proper' in marriage has been constructed at multiple levels of understanding. A close look at the texts may lead us to the Buddhist notion of the ideal conduct expected of married partners. We cannot overlook the fact that Jātakas had a clear intention to regulate the everyday lives of its lay followers. An intertextual study of the Jātakas, *Therīgāthā* and the *Theragāthā* might allow us to view the subtlety and the varied ways of constructing this ideal.

In one story from the Jātakas, a Bodhisatta was married to a lady of equal rank. [2] His family comprised of his wife, his children and a female slave. He used to support them by doing field labour. He asked his family members to be mindful of their mortal state and not dwell on death. With the passage of time, his son passed away and his wife, exhibiting perfect self-control, did not lament his death. However, Sakka asked the wife of the Bodhisatta how she was related to the dead man. On hearing that she was his mother, he was surprised. He asked her how she could face her irreparable loss. He said that a father owing to his manly nature would not weep, yet the mother's heart was always tender. He asked her with surprise, 'What then do you not weep?'[3] The gender identity of women in contemporary society is visible. She can weep and have a tender heart unlike her male counterpart. However, her compatibility with her husband in this instance is noticeable. She abides by his instruction and refrains from lamenting her son's death. This has been constructed as 'proper' in the narrative.

Often, supportive partners have been valorized as ideal for a balanced life. Thus, Buddhist narratives have a specific way of calculating merit with regard to qualities of empathy and support in companionship. This is perhaps a reflection of the Buddhist saṇgha, which is based on a cooperative ideology.[4] Supportive relations between couples can be identified as 'proper' in many instances from the Jātakas.[5] In one story a jackal couple killed an entire herd of goats except for a she-goat. The jackal asked his wife to befriend the she-goat and thus bring her to their feast. However, the goat proved to be intelligent and saved herself. Here we can trace the compatible partner in the she-jackal who tried to entice the she-goat by feigning friendship, following her male counterpart. In the above narrative the supportive relationship between the jackal duo is evident.

Besides the repeated construction of women in the stories as the reason of evil in marriage, there are occasional glimpses of 'proper' wives. This might be a deliberate way of creating a 'proper' model of a good wife. In the story of princess Sumedhā,[6] her father fixed her marriage with the son of his friend after her birth. As his daughter grew older his friend sent the king a marriage proposal to make Sumedhā his son's consort. However, her father said that he did not want his daughter to stay with the co-wives. He would give his daughter in marriage with a person who had no other wives. But the friend's son fell in love with Sumedhā on hearing about her peerless beauty. He decided to marry her and have no other wives. With the passage of time, no children were born to the couple. The townsfolk considered the queen barren and asked the king to marry again, but the king declined. The queen thought that this was because of his earlier promise that he would not marry again. She selected thousands of ladies from the warrior caste and presented them in marriage to the king, but none of them were able to bear sons. It was through the queen's prayer that Sakka was pleased and bestowed a son to her. The narrative hints at the compromising quality in the wife as a benevolent trait that could please even God.

Occasional representations of doting husbands surface in the representations of the Jātakas.[7] In one such tale a Bodhisatta was born as a monkey and lived on the bank of a river. A crocodile and his mate also lived in the river. Incidentally, the female crocodile desired to eat the heart of the monkey and asked her mate to get it for her. The monkey, through presence of mind, escaped from the crocodile's trap and saved his own life. In the above narrative, we find that the male crocodile is a supportive husband, who agreed to undergo any kind of hardship to fulfil the desires of his partner, despite his failure. Besides describing the male partner as a caring companion, the text has a subtle way of indicating the impossibility of fulfilling the absurd wishes of women.

A different situation features in another story from the Jātakas,[8] where a Bodhisatta was born to a Caṇḍāla woman in Benaras. His pregnant wife desired mangoes, without which she would not survive. Being infatuated with his wife the man trespassed into the king's garden to grab a mango. However, as the story progressed, the man realized his folly. He said to himself, 'I also am wicked, for I have fallen into the power of a woman, and counting my life as nought, I am stealing the mango fruit.'[9] Unlike the previous narrative of the crocodiles, here the man realized his 'mistake' in being kind to his wife. He understood that by supporting her whims he could have brought danger on himself. This narrative, in painting this behaviour as 'improper', is a caution to men about the consequences of being attentive to their wives' whims.

Interesting representations of supportive relations are developed in a narrative from the *Culla-Bodhi-Jātaka.*[10] A Bodhisatta was born to a brāhmaṇa's family in Benaras. When he grew up he was married to a maiden of the same status. However, neither of them desired married life. Even after marriage they never participated in any form of physical intimacy. After the demise of their parents, they decided to lead an ascetic life together. One day while sitting in a park, the king saw them. On seeing the beautiful lady the king fell in love with her. He asked the Bodhisatta how he was related to her. He said that in the worldly life she used to be his wife but at present she was his companion in the ascetic life. By exerting his sovereign power the king took the woman with him to his palace and gave her a position of high honour. With the passage of time the king realized that she was truly an ascetic and had no inclination towards worldly honour. He returned her to the Bodhisatta and asked them to stay in the park together. The above narrative portrays the detachment amicably practised by the couple in their married life as 'proper'. However, the husband remained so detached that even when the king abducted his wife he said she was no more a wife to him.

The verse of *therī* Ubbirī[11] is quite engaging. By acquiring merit she was reborn in the family of a very eminent person. Ubbirī was known for her beauty and was married to the king of Kosala. With the passage of time a daughter was born to them. The king was so glad to see the child he made Ubbirī his chief queen. However, their daughter died and the mourning mother renounced the world to become an ascetic. In this tale, the marriage between the king and Ubbirī was peaceful and 'proper'. She had all the worldly pleasures of being the chief queen and a mother. In a rare instance from these verses, the birth of a daughter was celebrated. Yet all these worldly attainments were futile when she realized the immense suffering of human bonding after the demise of her child. Later, she found solace after seeing the Master and renouncing the world.

A typical example of a selfish husband and a supportive wife has been represented in several stories from the Jātakas. On such story deals with a virtuous wife named Sambulā.[12] She was extremely beautiful and was married to prince Sotthisena. With the passage of time Sotthisena was affected by leprosy. One day he left his harem and decided to depart from his kingdom. Sambulā at once left the kingdom with him and took care of him in the forest. One day a goblin fell in love with her; however, she rejected all his advances. After hearing about this incident her husband tried to test her loyalty. He did not believe that she was innocent. However, by her virtue her husband was cured of leprosy. They returned to the kingdom and her husband was made the king. Although she was made his chief consort, in reality she had no honour as her husband still did not trust her loyalty. It was through the intervention of an ascetic that her husband realized his mistake and they lived happily after. In the narrative we come across the supportive wife of prince Sotthisena, who is a typical example of a 'proper' wife, followed her sick husband to the dangers of the unknown. Despite this, her husband was not only skeptical about her character but also refrained from bestowing any honours on her when he became the king. It was only at the end that he realized his mistake.

Another variant of this narrative is seen in the story of Brahmadatta, who reigned in Benaras.[13] One day the king found that his son, who served as his viceroy, had come to pay him respect. The king had a hunch that his son would be the reason for his destruction. Thus, he found it judicious to banish him from the kingdom, while the former was still alive. The prince, accompanied by his wife, went away and lived in the forest. Years later, when he came to know that his father had passed away, he planned to return to the kingdom. On the way his wife asked him 'Supposing, Sir, yonder mountain came into pure gold, would you give me some of it?' The prince said 'Who are you? I would not give you an atom'.[14] The woman then realized that although she had accompanied him in his solitude he was not ready to share his material acquisitions with her. On reaching Benaras, the prince was made the king and he established his wife in the position of chief queen; however, this was a mere titular rank and beyond it he paid her no respect. One day, the king's minster, a Bodhisatta, went to her and asked for a lump of rice. The queen stated that although she was the chief queen she didn't possess anything of her own so she couldn't even donate a lump of rice. Realizing her helpless state the Bodhisatta went to the king and reminded him of the queen's virtue. The king then became aware of his fault and bestowed powers on the queen.

The above narrative reveals the unequal relationship between the royal couple. The woman, like a true partner, accompanied her husband through uncertain times whereas her husband did not reciprocate her actions. He never considered her a partner in sharing his material possessions. Narratives like this can be compared to instances where women did not fit into the category of a 'proper' wife and the Master hardly intervened to amend their 'improper' ways, like he did in the case of their male counterparts.

If gratitude and companionship are held as expected qualities to postulate 'proper' marital relations, there are stories in the Jātakas that say otherwise. For instance, we hear the story of a miserly treasurer[15] who possessed wealth worth 80 crores but made no use of it either for his family or for himself. One day, on his way back home from the king's palace, the treasurer saw a country bumpkin eating cake stuffed with gruel. The sight aroused cravings within him but he thought that if he asked his wife to make the stuffed cake, he would have to share it with all the people of his household. He thought that this would cause him a lot of expenditure. Thus, he decided to not tell his wife. However, his wife, just by seeing him, understood that he craved something to eat. She discovered that her husband didn't want to have the stuffed cake out of fear of having to share it with others. So she told him that she would prepare a small number of cakes only for the two of them. The man disagreed and asked his wife not to make any for herself. To relieve her husband of his craving the wife immediately agreed to prepare the cakes only for him. To avoid everyone in the house she had to climb onto the rooftop to prepare the stuffed cake for her husband. Meanwhile, the Master sent the Elder Moggallāna to the miserly treasurer with the task of converting him. The Elder reached the treasurer's house, found the place where he was eating the cakes and asked for a share. After persistent denial failed to drive away the ascetic, the treasurer asked his wife to make a small cake to get rid of the sage. Accordingly, his obedient wife tried to make a very small cake but failed. Even the treasurer tried his hand but ended up making big cakes. Toiling over making a small cake for the sage made the treasurer lose his craving. He asked his wife to give the whole basket to the ascetic as he no longer wanted to have any cakes. The Elder then revealed the truth to the couple and disclosed his identity. As the story progressed, that the Elder asked the treasurer and his wife to come to the Buddha in the monastery and offer him the stuffed cakes. On reaching the Buddha and hearing his preaching, the treasurer lavished his wealth solely on the faith the Buddha taught. In the above narrative we get a picture of the treasurer's wife as a woman who was ready to undergo any ordeal to satisfy her husband's craving. Yet we don't see any reciprocity on the part of her miserly husband who was not even ready to give her a share of his meal.

Contrary to the above instance, examples of husbands who considered their wives to be natural shareholders in their possessions are also present in the Buddhist textual traditions. In many examples they are seen making their wives party to protecting their share of wealth from the rest of the world. In another narrative from the Jātakas, a fisherman cast his hook into the waters that were popular among his fellow fishermen.[16] A snag caught his hook and the fisherman thought it was a big fish. He sent his son to inform his wife and told her to quarrel with the rest of their family and keep them at home, so that there would be no one to share the fish with. Abiding by her husband's instructions, the wife began a quarrel with her neighbours. However, the quarrel took a serious turn and she was taken to the zamindar's court where she was severely penalized and beaten up.

In another story from the Jātakas we find the reflection of the compassionate female partner from the human world in the form of a doe.[17] A Bodhisatta was born as a stag with all the good qualities of a leader. He had a befitting companion in a beautiful doe. The two lived harmoniously together with the Bodhisatta's following of eight deer. A hunter set a snare in the forest. One day the Bodhisatta hurt himself badly, being entangled in the snare. Hearing him cry, the herd of deer fled in panic. However, the doe remained, boosting him with confidence and encouraging him to break the snare. Then, through her own power she succeeded in winning the heart of the hunter. She offered him her own life instead of the leader of the herd. The hunter was impressed with her and granted the life of the Bodhisatta. In this story we see that the doe was a true companion to the Bodhisatta. Not only did she keep on encouraging her partner, she was also ready to sacrifice her own life to save him.

A dichotomous representation of companionship in marriage is found in the words of a woman in a story from the Jātakas.[18] This woman begged the king for the release of her imprisoned husband, brother and son. She said that for a woman to be without a husband is equal to being without wealth; thus, she pleaded with the king to give back her wealth. The king was sympathetic towards her. He agreed to release one of her imprisoned relatives. The lady chose her brother and asserted that he was irreplaceable. She mentioned that on marrying again she would get a husband and a son. The king, impressed by her wisdom, released all the three men. This narrative interestingly presents the example of a woman who valued her husband like her wealth, without whom she was like an unclad person. While the woman valued her husband more than her wealth, she still cherished him less than her brother. Therefore when she had to make a choice, she chose her brother.

An unconventional understanding of 'proper' relations between a married couple surfaces in the verse of Abhayā.[19] By accumulating merit she was born in a great noble's family. She became the chief queen in the time of the Sikhi Buddha (the second of the seven Buddhas). One day it so happened that she met the Buddha while giving alms inside the palace. She immediately worshipped the Sikhi Buddha with the rose offered to her by the king. This enabled her to acquire merit and she was reborn in a respectable family. She later went on attain arhantship. While this verse acknowledges the warm gestures of the royal couple's expression of love, the tone in the commentary looks beyond these worldly ties. The *therī* in this particular verse can be seen worshipping the Sikhi Buddha with the rose she got from her husband. Here, almsgiving features as more important than such worldly gestures. Besides this, the story also hints at the close encounter of the royal household with the Brotherhood.

The best example of a husband as a companion features in certain stories from the Jātakas. This can be examined through the narrative of the only daughter of a rich merchant of Rājagriha, Lady Visākhā.[20] Despite leading a life of affluence we deduce that she had no interest in worldly life and desired to attain arhantship. However, as she was her family's only heir, she couldn't get permission from her parents to renounce her worldly life. It was only when she was married and pleased her in-laws with her virtues that she was permitted to renounce her material life. On one occasion her husband asked her to decorate her body. She told her husband that she would not do so and explained to him the stigmatized notion of the human body. Later, at her husband's initiative, she was admitted to the Order; however, at the time she was unaware that she was pregnant. Devadatta,[21] a contemporary of the Buddha, decided to expel her from the nunnery on hearing the news of her pregnancy. With the Buddha's intervention and with Visākhā's assurance about her pregnancy having commenced before her entering the ascetic life, she was allowed to stay in the nunnery and give birth to a son. This son was reared in the care of King Pasenadi's queens and when he grew to the age of seven he embraced a life of asceticism. The *therī*'s husband proved to be her true companion who felt her apathy for worldly existence and appreciated her earnest desire to renounce her material life.

A husband as a caring companion was a desired quality. This is evident in another story from the Jātakas where a Bodhisatta was born as a crow who was the chief of 80,000 other crows. His chief mate was very delicate.[22] One day she desired to have the king's food, and to fulfil this desire the chief crow sent his crew members to fetch the food. The crows were so dedicated to their master's orders that they acted according to plan and accomplished the mission. The king, learning about the loyalty in the crow kingdom, was so pleased that he gave them the same food that he ate. He also asked the Bodhisatta to impart his teachings to him. In the above narrative we come across the instance of true companionship between both partners.

Amicable terms between royal couples could be traced to the verse of *thera* Sīvali.[23] The mother of *thera* Sīvali was a princess and married into a royal household. During her gestation period she suffered for seven days. She told her husband that before she died she wanted to give him a gift. She sent him to meet the Master and narrate her sufferings to him. The Master blessed him and wished for the sound health of the royal lady and her child. On returning home the king saw a healthy child born to his queen. The commentary reveals that the royal couple invited the Buddha and the brethren to the palace and for seven days offered their hospitality to them. Here, the text hints at the cordial relation between the royal couple as 'proper'. The relation of dependence between the Buddhist Order and the king's palace is notable in this context.

The representation of conjugal life from the Jātaka stories is vast, and there is no homogeneity. In one narrative King Mahāpatāpa was reigning in Benaras when a Bodhisatta was born to him and the queen-consort Candā.[24] After his birth Candā spent most of her time taking care of him and exhibiting motherly affection towards him. This made the king jealous as he thought that his queen was oblivious of her duties towards him and remained so preoccupied with her child that she ignored the king's presence. This made Mahāpatāpa assume that when his son grew older, the queen would no longer remain loyal to him and would depend on her son. The king, in a fit of jealousy, thought of killing his own son so that the queen would remain a mere dependent on him her entire life. The queen, however, was ready to sacrifice her life to save her child from being butchered by the king's men but ultimately couldn't make the king yield to her pleadings. Acting according to the royal order, a servant cut off the child's hands and feet. Seeing this, the queen declared 'I will work for wages and support my son. Give him to me.'[25] Hearing this, the king killed his son, believing this would bring his wife back to him. However, the queen could not bear the pain of her son's death and died of sorrow. In this narrative the king could not come to terms with the fact that his wife had become occupied with her son. Being jealous, he murdered his son without considering his wife's attachment and emotions. Therefore, he failed to prove himself a compassionate partner.

Peaceful married life is also depicted in the verse of *therī* Soṇā[26] who was on amiable terms with her husband. This is evident in the fact that she followed him into the world of religion by cutting off her worldly ties. By accumulating merit she was born to an eminent family and later gave birth to many children, coming to be known as 'the Many-offspringed'. After her husband's renunciation from the world, she was not treated with respect by her children. In disdain she renounced the world and decided to follow her husband on the path of religion. Eventually, she handed over all her wealth and the household to her children and entered the saṇgha. In her verse she exclaims that her cultivated mind was completely free.[27] Here the text hints that severing ties with worldly life and being a partner to one's husband in religion is 'proper', as opposed to leading a life lacking respect with one's sons and daughters-in-law.

Examples of lay followers as supportive couples performing almsgiving were considered typical instance of 'proper' marital relations. One such story is of a Bodhisatta, who was born as a great merchant. He was very prosperous and sincerely performed almsgiving regularly.[28] Throughout the story the merchant's wife was his partner in the process of almsgiving. The merchant's extraordinary virtue and charity shook Sakka in heaven, who fell from his seat there.

He felt threatened by the merchant, believing that through his almsgiving, the merchant would earn merit and remove Sakka from his own position. He left no stone unturned in trying to turn the merchant into a pauper. Yet the Bodhisatta couldn't be stopped. He, along with his wife, sold grasses and performed almsgiving. Eventually, Sakka was pleased with the Bodhisatta and returned his wealth. Here, almsgiving has been constructed as a 'proper' gesture and the most noble virtue of any individual irrespective of social status.

Human behaviour is relative and can be explored through multiple possibilities. One such possibility is the treatment of a caring companion's wicked mate.[29] This is exemplified in the story of a country brāhmaṇa who was a student of a Bodhisatta and learnt the three Vedas and the eighteen sciences from him. He had a wicked wife who used to gad about all day and never did a stroke of work. She used to feign illness in the presence of her husband and made him toil like a slave. On hearing this, the Bodhisatta understood how evil his wife was. He told the brāhmaṇa that his wife was feigning illness and asked him not to provide his wife whatever she fancied. He suggested that the husband collect cow dung and ask his wife to swallow it to cure her illness. He also told the brāhmaṇa to ask his wife to work for her food if she refused to have it and to drag her by the hair and strike her with his fists. The brāhmaṇa acted as per the advice of his Master. As a result, the brāhmaṇa's wife realized that the Bodhisatta had intervened in the matter and it became impossible for her to deceive her husband. She got up and went about her work. She was conscious that the Master knew her wickedness; this made her repent and become as good as she had formerly been wicked. In this narrative the brāhmaṇa represents the obedient husband. He used to serve his wife as a naive servant. It was through the Master's intervention that he realized the wickedness of his wife and acted according to the advice of his master to remove her evil traits. In the story the husband resorts to physical violence. It is considered instrumental in making the 'wicked' wife conform to societal norms.

The working of marriage in the *Theragāthā* is typically portrayed through an aversion to domestic bonding. For instance, the verse of *thera* Vīra,[30] which has already been discussed in a different context in the previous chapter, would be referred to in this specific context. In his verse the married Vīra's firmness of character has been valorized as 'proper' as he turned down the 'improper' advances of his seductive wife. Another example along the same line surfaces in the verse of *thera* Puṇṇamāsa.[31] Puṇṇamāsa entered the Order after learning the four truths of the Buddhist faith. His wife from his worldly life tried to seduce him by dressing up and carrying their only son with her. Yet all her 'improper' endeavours proved futile in the face of the firm determination of the *thera*.

Perceptions Pertaining to the 'Improper' in Marriage

The idea of 'improper' relations in the Jātakas has been interwoven with conventional understandings of right and wrong in gender relations. As the structure of the Jātakas does not allow us to create a generalized idea of such conventions, I have discussed various examples of such case in a multitude of contexts below. Each case has a varied mechanism of dealing with right and wrong. The narratives are also entangled with the concern of Buddhist norms. However, through the examples discussed in this chapter, we will attempt to see the possibilities of nuanced relationships of and beyond the binaries of evil women and victimized men.

I have acknowledged that the Jātakas include multifaceted representations of marriages; thus, there is space available for extramarital relations in the stories. However, this possibility is considered anomalous within the textual representations. Paradoxically, it is seen that a woman with a lover or 'woman in love' is a matter of controversy who is inevitably demonized or portrayed as evil. On the contrary, a man having paramours even after marriage was more conventional. In these instances the blame at the end of the story invariably rests on his lover, who is often portrayed as wicked. These repeated representations of men being overpowered by the influence of beautiful women leaves one perplexed about the true nature of his willpower or self-control. The narratives hint at the immense power of women in captivating men, irrespective of their class and power. So immense was their power that they were shunned as a demons. They could lead ascetics astray and turn kings into imbeciles. Thus, it became an urgent need to fence them in with force. There are instances where women are beaten; Bodhisattas often instructed their disciples to do so. Their inborn 'evil' traits were either to be shunned or pardoned as they were beyond recovery. As a result, the allegation of the 'improper' in gender relations was mostly gender-specific.

The Jātakas explicitly recognize the need for men to maintain an optimum distance from the company of women. Women were perceived as adulterous by birth. It is held that there can be no means to tame the evil nature of women. In repeated representations in the stories, this notion becomes more clear.

The construction of the image of women with licentious tendencies was widespread.[32] The king of Benaras promised to grant his queen any boon she might request him. The queen asked him not to look at any other woman throughout his entire life. After some initial hesitation he submitted to the importunity of the queen. After that he never cast a glance of love at any of the women in his harem. Once, the king went to the frontier to handle the disturbed borderland and asked his queen to stay back in Benaras. He told her that battle camps were no place for a woman. However, in his absence, the queen sinned with the king's messengers. She also asked the Bodhisatta, the chaplain, to be intimate with her and fulfil her lust. On being repeatedly rejected by the Bodhisatta, the queen tried to take revenge on him. She feigned before the king that she was tortured by the Bodhisatta as she refused his approaches. The king burnt with rage and ordered his servants to cut off the Bodhisatta's head. As the story progressed, the Bodhisatta informed the king about the reality of the situation. He said that it was beyond his dignity to cast an eye of lust on another man's wife, let alone make love to her. He also revealed the previous sins of the queen to the king. Nonetheless, he asked the king to be merciful to the queen. He described the queen's sins as the innate nature of women, to which she was a victim. It is through this incident that the chaplain realized the futility of lay existence. With the king's permission he gave up his worldly life and became a recluse. In this tale the queen demanded the king to refrain from any relations with women. However, in her own life she could not practise the same. In the absence of the king, she involved herself in 'improper' relations with the king's messengers, throwing fidelity to the wind. It was only after approaching the Bodhisatta that she met with refusal. She tried to take revenge on the Bodhisatta but truth triumphed in the end. The king, on the advice of the Bodhisatta, pardoned her. It was ultimately the Bodhisatta who realized the futility of lay existence and renounced worldly life.

At times the inborn trait of unfaithfulness in women has resulted in punishment. We learn of an archer whose skill impressed the Master so much that he gave his daughter in marriage to the archer.[33] On their way to Benaras, the archer and his wife came across several perils. However, the archer resisted them all. The story took an interesting turn when they met a group of robbers. The archer asked his wife to bring his sword as he wanted to kill the robber chief. At that very moment she conceived passion for the robber chief. She gave the sword to the robber and got her husband killed. She narrated the story to the robber about how her husband was chosen by her father and because she fell in love with him, she let him kill her 'lawful husband'.[34] On hearing this the robber chief thought that any lady who could get her husband killed, would do the same to him if she liked any other man. He immediately thought of escaping from her and told her that he did not trust her. He believed that if passion took her she would forget about her 'well-tried faith' and pursue 'lighter love'.[35] Seeing the robber flee, the lady lamented the loss of both her husband and her lover. As the story ends we find that Sakka put her to shame. This particular narrative describes the infidelity of a wife as terribly 'improper'. She is accused of licentiousness to the extent that she loses both her husband and her lover at the same time. Though her lover had some initial inclinations towards her, he refrained from committing to her. He thought that a woman who has been unchaste once could repeat the same offence in the future.

An occasional hint of men being involved in relations outside wedlock can be seen in representations of Buddhist narratives. However, such story have sharply different momenta compared to the stories projecting women as adulterous. We hear of one such tale of a fowler, who remained engaged till late evening in disentangling his net.

However, the quails, his old prey, devised ways of escaping from his trap.[36] Thus, the man returned empty-handed every day. His wife began to suspect him of having another establishment with his lover where he spent his earnings. He explained the reality to his wife and said the birds had become united and thus were managing to escape. He assured her that when they start fighting with each other, he would be prosperous again. As the story ends we find that he managed to be fortunate again and bring happiness to his suspecting wife. The fowler predicted that the unity of the quails was temporary and that there would be in-fighting among them again. This is exactly what took place; the quails pushed each other while pulling the net, resulting in the shedding of their feathers. In this dilemma, none were able to escape. Thus, the fowler was able to capture them all and make a fortune selling his prey. In the narrative there is a clear hint at extramarital relationships being practised in society. This is reflected in the suspicion of the fowler's wife when he returned home without any earnings. However, unlike the earlier evidence of adulterous wives, we see that the man was falsely suspected by his wife.

The treatment of men having affairs outside wedlock varied from the stories where adulterous ladies were considered 'improper'. The construction of this gender bias was so subtly enmeshed in the gender relations of contemporary society that it appeared to be normal. This is apparent in the story of a treasurer's son.[37] His prolonged association with the brahma realm made his mind free from passion. During a festival his friends decided to send a charming girl to his room. They decked her up and sent her to his chamber. Nonetheless, he developed no intimacy with her and asked her to go back after taking some money from him. A conflict arose with the intervention of the girl's mother. She could not find her daughter anywhere and thus accused the treasurer's son of impropriety. As the story progresses, we see how the man realized the futility of lay existence and embraced asceticism. In this case the man had no interest in worldly passion but the narrative developed based on a certain tacit understanding where masculine promiscuity was regarded as conventional. This could be understood in the arrangement made by his friends. Enjoying life with a woman outside wedlock was not considered as a vice for the man in the social order of the time.

An interesting verse hinting at relations outside wedlock can be located in the instance of *therī* Ambapālī.[38] The conventional idea of royal men 'possessing' a courtesan has been reflected, and the understanding of the 'improper' is dubious here. After a series of rebirths Ambapālī was born at the foot of a mango tree and came to be known as the mango guardian's daughter. She gained worldwide fame because of her grace and charm. Many princes used to fight amongst each other to possess her. In order to end their strife she was made a courtesan of the town. She had sincere faith in the Master and donated a vihāra to him. Later she renounced the world following the preaching of her own son and realizing the impermanence of her bodily charm. The common understanding of married men having relations outside wedlock with courtesans was absent in the case of married women. No such convenient arrangement was meant for the latter.

Adultery as an 'improper' gesture features in the commentary of *thera* Ramaṇīyavihārin.[39] He was born to a wealthy household and was involved in youthful impiety. One day, on seeing an adulterer being arrested by the king's men, he became agitated and renounced the world. Yet the fleshly desire did not cease within him. He used to live in luxury but later left the place and roamed around. At some point of time he realized his faults and went to *thera* Upāli to absolve his faults and join the Order. In his *gāthā*, through a comparison to a brute of a noble breed who learns through his mistakes, he describes his experience of true insight in the noble path of the Buddha.[40]

In the story of King Brahmadatta from the Jātakas, the ruler fell in love with a woman who was singing in a garden. They became intimate and she eventually became pregnant with the Bodhisatta. The king gave her a signet ring and suggested she use the money obtained from such a piece of jewellery to bring up the child if it was a daughter. In case a son was born he should be sent to the king with the ring. As it happened, a son was born. The woman took her son to the palace with the ring, but the king refused to accept him. The lady had nothing to prove her child was the king's progeny as the latter did not accept the ring as proof of identity. However, when the child was recognized as the Bodhisatta, he was made the crown prince and his mother the queen consort. A close parallel to this popular narrative,[41] which emphasizes relations beyond marriage can be located in the verse about *thera* Abhaya's mother, the beautiful Padumavatī.[42] Yet, both narratives had different conclusions. She was renowned for her peerless charm and physical beauty and King Bimbisāra was enamoured with her. Later, she became pregnant with his child. Knowing this the king declared that she could send the child to him if it was a son. Incidentally, their son Abhaya was born and in his seventh year his mother sent him to King Bimbisāra. The king was affectionate to him and he was nurtured along with the other children of the royal household. Later, he started preaching dhamma. On hearing this Padumavatī lost interest in the world and renounced the worldly life. In these two narratives we come across relationships beyond wedlock. Unlike the Jātaka narrative the symbolic use of the signet ring is absent in the *Theravāda*. Despite this patriarchal way of favouring the birth of the son over the daughter, we can discern that marriage as a social contract was not emphasized in the verse. The entire idea of 'proper' and 'improper' has been constructed in a varied way in the verse.

The instance of *therī* Isidāsī is unique. She was beautiful and born to a wealthy family. She had suitors from all the noble families of Saketa and was finally married to a befitting family. She tried to please her in-laws in every possible way but failed to satisfy her husband. At one point he decided to part with Isidāsī and his parents sent her back to her home. They admitted that despite her good qualities akin to Goddess Lakṣmī, they were unable to convince their son to stay with her. Isidāsī described how her in-laws were sad to take her back to her parent's house—'*te maṃ pitugharaṃ paṭi nayiṃsu vimanā dukkhena avibhūtā puttam anurakkhamānā jitāmhase rūpiniṃ Lakkhiṃ*'.[43] Later, Isidāsī was married a number of times but each time it ended unsuccessfully. It was after meeting *bhikkhunī* Jinadattā that she wished to join the Order. Her father asked her to be a lay follower instead. Isidāsī recalled her past seven births and could trace the root of her misfortune to one of her past lives. In it, she was born a wealthy goldsmith and had intercourse with another man's wife. The sin was so severe that she never had a happy conjugal life in any of her marriages even in her rebirths. In one she was estranged from a husband of befitting status; in another she had tiffs with her husband's co-wives. Thus, in this context, the idea of 'proper' and 'improper' has been developed at varied levels of social existence.

The instance of *therī* Isidāsī brings up a number of issues. Once again the juxtaposition of different attitudes is revealed in the verse. Adulterous conduct was punishable by society. Her sin in her past birth as an adulterous man was the reason of her consecutive rebirths as a woman. No matter how dedicated she became to her husband she was never appreciated. The working of the theory of karma features in the description of her rebirths. Even when she became a devoted wife in one of her births, her husband is estranged from her. We come across her agitated self after repeated marriages have failed. At last, her sufferings end after she joins the Order.

In these texts, intimacy with women has been repeatedly projected as causing the downfall of men. A woman's power of influencing men has reached a level of fantasy in these representations. For instance, a Brother at Jetavana who was attracted to a plump young woman was ruined.[44] The Brother, intoxicated by the lady's charm, was made a fool of. Later, the Master told him that the lady was not of a decent character as in his previous birth (where he was born as a pig), she had fed him to the guests at her wedding. Here, the Master visualizes the man's desire for the plump woman as 'improper' and narrates to him the story of his past existence, where he was a pig and fattened with food, only to be butchered in a festival.

A *purohita* in Benaras used to lose money regularly while playing dice with the king. He decided to rear a newborn girl in his custody so that she could never come in contact with men.[45] However his mission remained unaccomplished. The girl he reared in tight confinement could hardly be kept away from committing sin. With the passage of time she developed intimacy with a man and made him her paramour. Associating with her lover, she made a fool of the *purohita*. A Bodhisatta told the *purohita* that no matter what and how one protected a woman, she could never be kept away from adultery. He said that it was foolish to trust women as they were born with innate sins. Here, the man's attempt to tame a woman has been stigmatized as 'improper' and futile. An emphasis on her affair with her lover and escaping from the *purohita* was deliberately made to hint at the disloyal traits in women.

Unsurprisingly, the construction of the image of the unfaithful female partner was a recurrent theme in several Buddhist narratives. Take the example of a mountain stag and a doe. The mountain stag, being attached to a doe, came down the mountain. The doe warned him of all the possible dangers on the way.[46] Yet he turned a deaf ear to all the warnings and accompanied her down the hill. Sensing the presence of a hunter, the doe let the stag proceed first and she followed him at a considerable distance. As a result, the hunter killed the stag with his arrow and the doe escaped immediately. A Bodhisatta was a fairy in a nearby grove. He stated that it was his 'improper' desire that brought about the untimely death of the stag. The stag was deemed to be a fool as he yielded to female domination. In the above narrative intimacy and affection without being critical is severely admonished as 'improper', and the Bodhisatta states that women are born traitors and yielding to them would lead one astray.

The image of a woman as an evil partner and the labelling of marriage as 'improper' by the Master can be discussed in a narrative from the Jātakas.[47] A brāhmaṇa was the pupil of a Bodhisatta. He became intimate with a woman and made her his wife. After getting married he failed to live in peace. His wife used to sin and behaved unpredictably. Sometimes she remained meek and servile while on other days she was passionate and tyrannical. The brāhmaṇa told the Master that it was because of his wicked wife that he could not meet him anymore. The Master told him that women were hard to predict and asked him not to pay heed to the likes and dislikes of his wife. He also mentioned that by falling for the woman, he had been repeating the same sin he committed in his previous birth.

Situations took different turns where men could ignore the desire of beautiful women.[48] In one such story the 'improper' gestures of a woman were not entertained by *thera* Samiddhtheraṁ.[49] Realizing his disinterest, she vanished. This narrative surfaces as an example of a man with a 'proper' outlook and judicious mindset who could avoid the improper advances of a woman and attain peace.

Marriages are supposed to be relations based on choice as we do not inherit these on birth. As discussed in the previous chapter, matrimonial ties have little to do with the choice of the individuals concerned. Yet, there are rare portrayals of individuals falling in love and getting married or falling in love outside nuptial ties. In both the cases and even cases beyond these binaries, situations perceived as 'improper' were common. Infidelity in marriages giving way to physical abuse is occasionally visible in the representations of the Jātakas. We learn of a woman who was involved in an adulterous relation with her paramour in the absence of her husband.[50] Realizing his own mistake the brāhmaṇa beat his wife and her lover, teaching them a lesson that they would never forget. At the end of the story, he abandons worldly life.

Relations with 'other women' were not rare instances in the representations of the Jātakas. In the story from the *Kanavera-Jātaka*,[51] we come to know of a courtesan Sāmā, known for her high price and charm, who was the king's favourite. Once she fell in love with a robber and decided to give up her profitable trade and marry him. She went to the extent of betraying one of her loyal clients to save the life of the robber. As the story went on, we see that the robber betrayed her. He was apprehensive that the *gaṇikā* (courtesan) would cheat him when she found another man, in the same way that she cheated her previous client for him. One day, he robbed her and ran away never to come back again, in spite of her ardent pleas. With regret, she reverted back to her trade.

In the above narrative the conflict in Sāmā's relations becomes clear. The courtesan betrayed a loyal client and broke his trust for someone with whom she had no former acquaintance. She fell for him, ignoring the fact that he was a robber. At the end of the story, the robber could not trust the courtesan who betrayed her regular client and wanted to marry him. He robbed her of her wealth and ran away. We see that after a period of grief she returned to her old profession. In this narrative, the textual perception of the 'improper' gesture in violating her trade norms is apparent. We see how she was mistrusted by the person she desired to marry and was cheated by him. Her returning back to the old profession is symbolic of the contemporary societal norms that a prostitute could be company to many but a wife to no one.

Unlike the previous story, the tale of the courtesan Sulasā, in the *Sulasā-Jātaka*, is defensive in nature. In this narrative[52] a courtesan named Sulasā fell in love with a robber and wished to marry him. As the story progresses we learn that the robber took advantage of her and planned to kill her. However, Sulasā realized his intentions and murdered him before he could kill her and returned to the city.

In both the above narratives the conflict stems from the courtesan's unconventional desire for a man and her wish to marry him. The textual tone indeed portrays this desire as 'improper' as it is the root of a series of conflicts. An interesting paradoxical situation crops up in this context, where a prostitute who was desired by many and was praised for her charm was penalized of desiring a man of her choice. Many of the narratives cited before pointed at married women who were licentious and had paramours outside wedlock; however, their publishment was not as severe. These instances show powerful ladies like courtesans occasionally desiring husbands and marriage, flouting their trade rules. The Buddhist texts show the audiences examples of the courtesan's failed attempts. They were either cheated and shown their place or they joined the Buddhist saṇgha. However, not a single instance spoke in favour of their desires getting fulfilled.

The treatment of 'other woman' as an articulate entity was evident in the representations of the Jātakas.[53] One such story deals with a certain beautiful courtesan in Benaras. Once, a young merchant who was a regular visitor came to her while he was penniless. The courtesan immediately turned him down and said that she did not serve anyone who was empty-handed. The man was disappointed as even after spending a huge sum of 80 crores on her, she refused to serve him for even one day without money. He realized the wickedness of womankind and, feeling betrayed, decided to abandon the layman's life. However, the king, who was a close friend of the merchant punished her and asked her to bring the man back. However, the merchant had lost all interest in worldly life and was living as an ascetic. On finding him in the forest, the courtesan begged him for forgiveness. The man forgave her but did not return to his worldly life. On hearing the same, the king decided to forgive the courtesan's sins.

The occasional representation of the articulate female—often typified by the courtesan—can be discerned in the above story. The conflict between the courtesan and her client is noteworthy; her stern professionalism has been described as heartless and rude. Her turning down of her client is portrayed as wickedness. Her 'improper' gesture was enough to make her client to give up his worldly life.

A similar instance of conflict between human couples could be traced to another story from the Jātakas.[54] Here, the story narrates the anxiety between a royal couple regarding their newborn infant. The king became jealous as the queen was busy with the newborn and could no longer devote the same amount of time or show the same amount of care and concern for him. As a result, he orders his own son to be killed. A contradictory image of this 'improper' gesture by the king is seen in that of the queen. She is ready to give up her royal status for the sake of her son. She says that she will protect the life of her son and support him by earning money by herself.

More serious ruptures occur in the social fabric of the time, with the relationships between good and evil characters having long-term consequences in families and in society in general.[55] In one such story we hear of a Bodhisatta being reborn as a golden bird called Suvaṇṇahaṁsa.[56] After his death his wife and daughters were living on charity and leading a miserable life. Suvaṇṇahaṁsa started visiting them and gave them his golden feathers to enable them to earn a better living. With the passage of time his wife earned a lot by selling his feathers. One day, she decided to take away all Suvaṇṇahaṁsa's feathers and gain some quick and easy earnings. However, none of his feathers remained gold as they were taken without his consent. This narrative is another variant describing marriage as 'improper' by pointing to women as evil characters. The conflict between the married partners is evident even after the death of the spouse. Here there is an interesting juxtaposition of human and bird characters. In this story the Bodhisatta was reborn as a brāhmaṇa and, after his death, was once again reborn as a golden mallard. The story is interesting because it describes human and non-human associations. A bird, remembering its human responsibilities from a past birth, tries to perform them with sincerity. However, this righteous behaviour puts him in a life-threatening situation by the inhuman behaviour of his wife.

Perceptions of the 'improper' in woman were very common in representations of gender relations.[57] The construction of 'bad' women as a category has been generalized. The Master, while making a Brother aware of the evil traits in women, said that women could not be guarded or kept safe even under iron-tight restrictions. He mentioned that even in earlier times sages placed women in the midst of the ocean to guard them, but failed.

Interestingly, the evil traits of women are at times treated as more heinous than demons. Let us focus on a specific narrative[58] of a demon who failed in the face of a maiden's wickedness. In the story, the demon fell in love with a maiden and carried her off to his cave after making her his wife. He was so protective of her that he put her in a box and swallowed it so that she could not escape. Once, before leaving to bathe, he removed the box from his stomach and asked his wife to enjoy the open air. In his absence, Vayu, the magician, who was passing over the area, was enticed by the woman, who trapped him in the box with her. The demon swallowed the box, unaware that there were two people inside. When he went to visit the Bodhisatta, he was alarmed to be told that Vayu was inside his belly. Scared of Vayu's tricks, the demon the removed the box and threw it away. Vayu took this opportunity to escape, sword in hand.

The demon thanked the Bodhisatta for saving his life and was wrathful at his wife's betrayal. However, the Bodhisatta asked him not to do her any harm, after which the demon, realizing the impossibility of expecting such degree of loyalty from a woman, let her go.

In another story, a Bodhisatta found a young girl in a lotus and adopted her as his daughter. The daughter was born with auspicious marks.[59] The Bodhisatta raised her with care and she grew up into a woman with unparalleled beauty. The king of Benaras, on hearing of her beauty, wanted to possess her. He went to the Bodhisatta to gain the hand of his beautiful daughter. The Bodhisatta told him that he could take the maiden only if he knew her name. A year passed but he could not find out her name and decided to leave. On seeing the maiden at the window, the king told her that he could not discover her name and so had decided to return to Benaras. She told the king that he would never find a wife as good as her. She also told him that he should not be discontented and impatient. The king was impressed by her words and made fresh attempts at guessing her name. However, he failed this time as well. A year passed, after which he decided to go back to Benaras. However, she managed to influence him once again and he stayed back, failing repeatedly. After his repeated failures, the king told her that she could attract and impress him with her words but not with love; hence, he would depart. However, the king at last managed to guess her name and took her as his wife. Taking her father's permission, she departed with the king. In this narrative the king is attracted by the maiden's beauty. Yet, he was impatient about the price he was supposed to pay for the same. At one point he realized that though he was impressed by her charm, she could not satisfy him with love.

The complexities in gender relations and repeated discussions on the 'improper' nature of women surface on multiple levels. In a story from the *Culla-Palobhana-Jātaka*[60] there is conflict regarding the relation between a prince and a dancing girl. From his childhood the prince detested the company of women; this worried his father. On hearing this, a dancing girl from the city approached the king and said she could help him with his son. She set the condition that if she was able to make the prince fall in love with her, the king would marry her to the prince and make her a princess. She succeeded in seducing the prince and he gradually became very possessive of her. Desire arose in him and he would chase anyone who sought her company. Seeing his insane behaviour, the king banished him from the city. There they lived happily until the girl met an ascetic and seduced him. The prince, imagining the ascetic to be his foe, chased him with his sword brandished. However, the ascetic rose into the sky like a piece of cotton. Seeing this, the prince became attracted towards an ascetic lifestyle; he let go of the girl and practised a life of meditation in the jungle.

Parting with bad company as the ultimate solution to regular domestic conflict is observed in a story from the *Udaṇcani-Jātaka*.[61] A Bodhisatta asked his son about his consecutive absence from meetings where the Buddha would preach his discourse to his folowers. His son replied that in the absence of the Bodhisatta, he was lured by a woman. He said that the lady had been waiting for him because he was not ready to leave the hermitage without the permission of his father. The Bodhisatta recognized his son's passion and asked him to leave with his partner. He told his son that the moment the latter he was being used by his partner, he should come back to the hermitage. With the passage of time, the son realized his mistake. He understood how badly his partner had taken advantage of him. Finally, he parted with her and returned to the hermitage. In the above narrative we see the Bodhisatta making accurate predictions regarding the conflict if his son got married to his lover. He was assured of this to the extent that he told his son to return to the hermitage if he faced any conflict of interest. This story is told in hermitages, where the audiences were specifically monks. Discouraging marriage is the main theme of the narrative. What is noticeable is that the institution of marriage is discouraged by vandalizing the image of women in general.

The selfish (female) partner also features in a story from the *Padakusalamāṇava Jātaka*.[62] A woman was with her husband, a dancer named Patala, when times were good. He made his living by dancing and singing and they enjoyed their life together. One day, he earned a handsome amount of money and spent it on strong drinks. He soon fell unconscious and dropped his flute in the river. When he came to his senses, he brought his wife to the river and walked into it to find his flute. However, when he began to sink, his wife let him go and stood on the bank. As he was about to die, she asked him to teach her one song so she could sustain herself when he was gone. Thus, during this time of distress, she exhibited her selfishness by asking the man to teach her a song which she could utilize in earning her livelihood in his absence. This narrative stands sharply in contrast to the 'proper' supportive relations portrayed between married partners.

Instances of the charm of seductive women failing to entice Brothers is quite common in the Buddhist textual traditions. *Therī* Vimalā[63] was born to a courtesan. One day she saw the venerable Mahā-Moggallāna and was enamoured by him. She went to his dwelling and tried to entice him using her 'improper' charms. However, she failed to do so and was admonished by him. She was so ashamed of her 'improper' deeds that she became a lay sister after self-reflection. Rumour spread after this incident that the lady who went to seduce the Brother was instigated by sectarian religions. The above commentary opens before us a plethora of issues. Although it is not mentioned that the daughter of the courtesan followed the same profession, she grew up to become a seductress who could be hired to entice men. Here we are presented with an image beyond the conventional understanding of men being enticed by the charm of beautiful women; on the contrary, the woman in this verse was enamoured by the venerable Mahā-Moggallāna. What followed this was notable. Indeed, the *thera* was not labelled a seducer; instead, one finds a typical narrative about the lady being a professional seductress. She was the one enamoured by him and went to entice him. However, she ended up being admonished by the venerable Brother.

Another example along the same line surfaces in the verse of *thera* Puṇṇamāsa.[64] Learning the four truths of the Buddhist faith, he entered the Order. His wife from his worldly life tried to seduce him by adorning herself and by carrying their only son along with her. Yet all her 'improper' endeavours proved futile in the face of the firm determination of the *thera*.

In the *Theragāthā*, the evidence of wives seducing their husbands is frequent. In the verse of *thera* Posiya,[65] we learn that after his child was born he renounced the world and began residing alone in the forest. After attaining arhantship he came back to see his family. His wife entertained him and tried to draw him back to his worldly life. Because of his wife's 'improper' gestures, he realized that desire was aiming to submerge him. Thus, he took a 'proper' step to get back to the Order as early as possible. Here we can clearly visualize the inclination of the text against physical pleasures. The construction of 'proper' and 'improper' behaviour has been done according to these inclinations.

The portrayal of a *thera* taking interest in married life and enjoying worldly life is rare. Yet we get such hints in the commentary on the verse of *thera* Hārita.[66] He enjoyed his married life with his wife and remained enamoured by her physical charm. It was only after her demise from a snake bite that Hārita realized the impermanence of worldly life. Without any hesitation he severed all his domestic ties and renounced the world. In this verse we see him suffering for his 'improper' gesture of being lured by his wife after her death.

Another example of the hardships of married life features in the verse of *theri* Kisā-Gotamī.[67] She was reborn into a poor family of Sāvatthī. She was known as 'lean Gotamī' because she was thin and was treated disdainfully after her marriage. However, after the birth of a son, she was shown some respect. As the commentary progressed, we learn that her little son died and she became maddened with grief. It was after seeing the Master that she realized the futility of worldly ties. Friendship with the Buddha made her attain wisdom and freed her from suffering. On attaining arhantship, Gotamī reflected on the great things she had learnt in the process. She mentioned the vices of worldly existence. In one verse, a female deity speaks to her about the state of being a woman and the pain of a married life that had to be shared with one's co-wives. A female deity surfaces who narrated the woes of co-wives of one's husband.

In the narrative, *therī* Kisā-Gotamī described the hardships of another woman named Paṭācārā who went through a terrible time while delivering her child. Paṭācārā lost her husband, and her children also eventually passed away. Gotamī also spoke about her own sufferings and hardships as a woman. It was only by following the eightfold path that she could be liberated.[68]

These examples of the 'improper' in marriage reveal the plurality in the understanding of social life. The '*ucca kula*' (upper echelon of society) and '*nīca kula*' (lower echelon) appear as sharp demarcations in defining the contextual differences of the 'improper' in marriages. In the *Theragāthā* the portrayal of social life as malevolent has been constantly suggested by labelling the wives of *bhikkhus* as seductresses. It has been pointed that the wives engaged in seducing their husbands to bring them back to the social world are 'improper'. On the contrary a *bhikkhunī* is never seen experiencing such persuasion from her husband.

In this section there have been several narratives suggesting adulterous relations. In each of the cases then women have been pointed out as adulterers and punished for the same. However, in the same narratives the projection of men being involved in relations beyond nuptial ties was limited to a mere suspicion on the part of their foolish wives. Included in the construction of a 'good wife' was her tolerance of her co-wives. Another interesting feature in the structural difference in the stories of the Jātakas on one hand and the *Therīgāthā* and the *Theragāthā* on the other hand is the fact that the Jātakas have a unique way of narrating a story of the Buddha's present birth where the Master, in the beginning of the story, refers to the mistakes committed by a person in his previous birth. He warns the person of the consequences faced by him there. However, in the *Therīgāthā*, the instances of the present birth are described as a consequence of the sin or merit from the previous birth of the *therī*. Interestingly, in most instances from the *Theragāthā*, *bhikkhus* are reborn due to the merits accumulated in their past births. These stand sharply in contrast to the sins committed by most of the *therīs* in their earlier lives. It was only by donating generously to the saṇgha that some of the *therīs* could manage rebirth into a better life. It is also interesting that the perception of women/wives as potentially evil is a common strand in both the Jātakas and the *Theragāthā*. The *Therīgāthā*, on the other hand, does not condemn 'improper' men in the same way. Thus, overarching concerns and understandings of the gender hierarchy are apparent in these differing narrative strategies.

Conclusion

It can be said by way of conclusion that the main theme in the narratives discussed in this chapter revolve around the everyday life of people. What is striking is the range of situations we come across in the stories. Besides companionship, the marriages in these narratives reflect the complexities and varied nature of gender relations. There are also instances where such relations from the human world are also reflected in the animal world. In one such example, some birds mock another bird who laments the demise of his beloved wife. This is clearly reflective of the situation in the human world. Such varied instances in the Buddhist texts regarding nuptial ties allow us to look at gender relations in the social sphere in more than one way.

In the Jātakas, supportive husbands do not have happy endings; instead, they end up as victims. On the contrary, a supportive wife at the beck and call of her husband is the 'proper' image of an ideal wife. Instances of the Master's intervention to reform or correct the derailed or insensitive husband and bring him back onto the right track is absent unlike the case of wives portrayed as 'improper' partners in marriages. However, the *Therīgāthā* and the *Theragāthā* visualize exemplary partnerships as couples renouncing worldly life and joining each other in religious pursuits. Simultaneously, dedicated lay followers among couples who supported the saṇgha were always appreciated.

In this chapter we also see also evidence suggesting adulterous relations. In each of the cases the woman has been pointed out as the adulterer and punished for the same. However, the narrative's projection of men being involved in adulterous relations was limited to the mere suspicion of their unreasonable wives. Besides, an idea of a 'good wife' included tolerance of her co-wives.

Unlike the normative texts (like the *Vinaya Pitaka*) there was no particular emphasis in the Jātakas, *Therīgāthā* or *Theragāthā* on the construction of 'right' and 'wrong'. Instead, there are varied instances of 'proper' and 'improper' behaviour. The Jātakas encompass a variety of possibilities in the understanding of the 'proper' and the 'improper' in the working of marriages, resulting in open-ended narratives that look beyond bipolar assumptions. In contrast, the *Therīgāthā*—through each of the verses attributed to the nuns— intends to show that all worldly sufferings are 'improper' and can be overcome by adopting the 'proper' means of renouncing the world. However, the *Theragāthā* is more specifically about the *bhikkhus*, with a focus on their experience in the saṇgha. It seems relatively easy for them to follow the 'proper' way with the guidance of the Master. Thus, it can be discerned that Buddhist principles played a catalystic role in channelizing the lives of the *theras*. The portrayal of the past lives of the *theras* has a Buddhist principle of monitoring and channelizing ideas.

A comparative study of these texts brings forth evidence pointing to a deep concern with conjugal relations. The ideological intervention of the Master into the private spaces of couples is extended. The narrative strategy in each of the texts successfully reveals the 'proper' and 'improper' elements in conjugal life as per Buddhist ethics. The verses exemplify the Buddhist principle of visualizing the 'proper' and 'improper' in nuptial ties. It is beyond doubt that Buddhism was antithetical to conventional tradition and was one of the protestant religions. Yet how far it actually redefined the androcentric and patriarchal biases of society is questionable. A persistent attempt at negotiating the differences between the social and asocial world and providing a possibility of an alternative structure in the saṇgha is also noticeable in these narratives. The perception of the 'proper' and 'improper' within the Buddhist ethos was based on several worldly factors like kingship, lay disciples and other heterodox sects. The 'improper', especially in the Jātakas, is often visualized in terms of violating hierarchies of class and gender. In the *Therīgāthā* and *Theragāthā* on the other hand, most marriages were by definition regarded as improper. The coexistence of these diverse possibilities within the canonical Buddhist tradition indicates that the social world within which the tradition developed was complex and diverse.

NOTES

1. Kunal Chakrabarti, 'Brahmanical Hegemony and Oppressed Social Groups: Rethinking the "Kaivartta Revolt"' in *Early Indian History and Beyond*, ed. O. Bopearachchi and Suchandra Ghosh, New Delhi: Primus Books, 2019.
2. E.B. Cowell, ed.,The Jatakas, New Delhi: Munshiram Manoharlal, 2002, *Uraga-Jātaka*, story no. 354. All references to the Jātakas are from this translation.
3. Ibid., p. 109.
4. There are certain benchmarks in the Buddhist way of attaining merit. One of the most basic amongst these is cooperating with and supporting each other. A supportive partner or companion is always valorized in the Buddhist textual traditions.

5. Cowell, *Pūtimaṅsa-Jataka*, story no. 437.
6. Cowell, *Suruci-Jātaka*, story no. 489.
7. Cowell, *Vānarinda Jātaka*, story no. 57.
8. Cowell, *Chavaka-Jataka*, story no. 309.
9. Ibid., p. 309.
10. Cowell, *Culla-Bodhi-Jātaka*, story no. 443.
11. Davids, *Psalms of the Early Buddhists*, canto 3, commentary XXXIII, verse 17.
12. Cowell, *Sambula-Jātaka*, story no. 519.
13. Cowell, *Succaja Jātaka*, story no. 320.
14. Ibid.
15. Cowell, *Illīsa Jātaka*, story no. 78.
16. Cowell, *Ubhatobhaṭṭha Jātaka*, story no. 139.
17. Cowell, *Suvaṇṇamiga Jātaka*, story no. 359.
18. Cowell, *Ucchaṅga Jātaka*, story no. 67.
19. Davids, *Psalms of the Early Buddhists*, canto 2, commentary XXVII, verse 35–6.
20. Cowell, *Nigrodhamiga Jātaka*, story no. 12.
21. While Devadatta was the Buddha's contemporary, he also had his own followers and nurtured a hostile relationship with the saṅgha.
22. Cowell, *Supatta Jātaka*, story no. 292.
23. Davids, *Psalms of the Early Buddhists*, canto 1, part V, commentary LX, verse 60.
24. Cowell, *Culladhammapāla Jātaka*, story no. 358.
25. Ibid.
26. Davids, *Psalms of the Early Buddhists*, canto 5, commentary XLV, verse 102–6.
27. See Hallisey, tr., *Therīgāthā*, verse 105.
28. Cowell, *Visayha Jātaka*, story no. 340.
29. Cowell, *Kosiya Jātaka*, story no. 130.
30. Davids, *Psalms of the Early Buddhists*, canto 1, part I, commentary VIII, verse 8.
31. Davids, *Psalms of the Early Buddhists*, canto 1, part I, commentary X, verse 10.
32. Cowell, *Bandhanamokkha-Jātaka*, story no. 120.
33. Cowell, *Culladhanuggaha-Jātaka*, story no. 374.
34. Ibid., p. 146.
35. Ibid.
36. Cowell, *Sammodamāna Jātaka*, story no. 33.

37. Cowell, *Vaṭṭaka-Jātaka*, story no. 118.
38. Rhys Davids, *Psalms of the Early Buddhists*, London: Pali Text Society and New York: Luzac and Co., 1964, cantos 13, commentary LXVI, verse 252–70.
39. Ibid., canto 1, part V, commentary XXIV, verse 45.
40. H. Oldenberg and R. Pischel, *The Thera- and Theri-gatha (Stanzas Ascribed to Elders of the Buddhist Order of Recluses)* (online version), London: Pali Text Society, 1883, verse 45, see http://gretil.sub.uni-goettingen.de/gretil/2_pali/1_tipit/2_sut/5_khudd/theragou.htm, accessed 10 April 2016.
41. Cowell, *Jātakas*, story no. 7.
42. Davids, *Psalms of the Early Buddhists*, cantos 2, commentary XXVI, verse 33–4.
43. See Charles Hallisey, tr., *Therīgāthā: Poems of the First Buddhist Women*, London: Murty Classical Library of India, 2015, verse 422.
44. Cowell, *Muṇika Jātaka*, story no. 30.
45. Cowell, *Aṇḍabhūta-Jātaka*, story no. 62.
46. Cowell, *Kaṇḍina Jātaka*, story no. 13.
47. Cowell, *Durājāna Jātaka*, story no. 64.
48. Cowell, *Samiddhi-Jātaka*, story no. 167. For a detailed discussion see Chapter 2.
49. See V. Fausboll, ed., *The Jātakas Together with its Commentaries*, vol. 1, London: Trubner & Co., 1877–96, p. 56, story no. 167.
50. Cowell, *Ucchiṭṭha-Jātaka*, story no. 212.
51. Cowell, *Kanavera-Jātaka*, story no. 318.
52. Cowell, *Sulasā-Jātaka*, story no. 419.
53. Cowell, *Aṭṭhāna-Jātaka*, story no. 425.
54. Cowell, *Culladhammapāla Jātaka*, story no. 358.
55. Cowell, *Suvaṇṇahaṁsa Jātaka*, story no. 136.
56. See Fausboll, *The Jātakas Together with its Commentaries*, story no. 136.
57. Cowell, *Kākāti-Jātaka*, story no. 327.
58. Cowell, *Samugga Jātaka*, story no. 436.
59. Cowell, *Āsaṅka-Jātaka*, story no. 380.
60. Cowell, *Culla-Palobhana-Jātaka*, story no. 263.
61. Cowell, *Udañcani-Jātaka*, story no. 106.
62. Cowell, *Padakusalamāṇava Jātaka*, story no. 432.
63. Davids, *Psalms of the Early Buddhists*, canto 5, commentary XXXIX, verse 72–6.

64. Ibid., canto 1, part I, commentary X, verse 10.
65. Ibid., canto 1, part IV, commentary XXIV, verse 34.
66. Ibid., canto 1, part III, commentary XXIX, verse 29.
67. Ibid., canto 10, commentary LXIII, verse 213–23.
68. See Hallisey, tr., *Therīgāthā*, verse 222.

3

The Household

Contextualizing Marriage and 'Beyond'

'SOCIAL SPACE IS a social product' is an overarching understanding of space suggested by Henri Lefebvre. Social space incorporates social actions of subjects as individual and collective, contextualized in a space which they either enjoy or modify. Space is a phenomenon produced by society and hierarchies become part of this social space. My purpose here is to comprehend how households are structured within the Buddhist texts and how individuals are located within it. The representation of the household in the Buddhist textual tradition has a number of aspects. On one hand this representation is often determined by existing social realities. On the other hand, the purpose of these texts is also to influence the society in return.[1]

The early Buddhist traditions consider the household as a repository of suffering. The Jātakas, which portray the previous births of the Buddha, in many instances effectively exhibit the intense hurdles of domesticity. The Buddhist textual narratives do not directly condemn worldly households as the womb of all discontent. Instead, they adopt a pragmatic way of describing situations in the social sphere to which solutions can only be found by renouncing the world. At this juncture the description of the possibility of an alternative situation exemplified by the saṇgha is portrayed in the *Therīgāthā* and the *Theragāthā*. However, the Buddha's reluctance to admitting women to the Order is evident in these textual traditions. It was only at the initiative of his disciple Ānanda that women were permitted to join the saṇgha, abiding by the gendered rules.

My objective in this chapter is to explore the images of domesticity and relations of hierarchy and dependence within the household. The household often becomes the spatial ground for social dyads bound through nuptial ties; hence, it becomes important to understand the paraphernalia of different households. Understanding the rituals and traditions of various households may allow us to locate the social context of marriages and relations of hierarchy stemming from them. The discussion in this chapter will develop under two broad themes: the structural paradigm of the household and 'beyond' and relations of dependence and hierarchy within the household and beyond it.

Structural Paradigm of the Household and 'Beyond'

Marriage is the most significant ritual that initiates an individual into the life of a householder. Yet, Buddhism, with its emphasis on the importance of liberation, represents a different position on the worldly ties of the household. The stories of the Buddha's previous birth contain varied images of worldly existences through which we come across different households that can be broadly categorized as elite and those of ordinary people. Through the representation of different rituals and traditions the extent of equity in gender roles within the household can be understood. On the one hand the lay household can be seen gaining merit by generously supporting the Buddhist saṇgha. On the other hand, the description of the household as synonymous with all the complexities and miseries of wordly existence was common. This foregrounds the saṇgha as an alternative possibility 'beyond' the life of a householder, sustained by the donations of lay followers.

Gendered Roles within the Household

Here I will scrutinize gender relations in nuptial ties in order to understand the foundation of social life within the household. Certain issues have been questioned and answered accordingly: did both partners have an equal presence in every aspect of household traditions? What were the differences in accessibility of space based on gender? How did the same space adhere to the different lived experiences of the people situated within it?

The royal household was the predominant model of the household in society. To begin discussing the rituals and traditions in the king's home, we will first focus on narratives from the Buddhist texts that expemplify ceremonies regarding childbirth. In one story from the Jātakas a Bodhisatta was in a royal household of the queen consort of King Brahmadatta in Benaras.[2] The story introduces us to certain rituals that followed the birth of the royal child, including the naming ceremony, where the little prince was named Prince Brahmadatta. Eventually, he was sent to Takkasilā to train and to gain an education. By the age of 16 he was well versed in the knowledge of the three Vedas. On returning home, he was placed in the coveted position of viceroy by his father. The prince was worried about the religious beliefs of the people in Benaras as the chief means of worship was animal sacrifice. On his tour around the city he saw that people were worshipping a holy banyan tree, praying to the female spirit for offspring. After the death of his father, Brahmadatta was made the king. He told his subjects that he was a fervent worshipper of the banyan tree and thus was made the king. He added that he had vowed to the tree that if his wish was fulfilled, he would make an offering to God. He asked his ministers to spread the news throughout the city that the king would offer a sacrifice to the tree by killing people who were unrighteous and practised animal slaying. After this news spread like wildfire, there was not a single person who practised animal sacrifice. Thereafter, the practice of animal sacrifice ceased to exist in the city. In this narrative the picture of the royal household unfolds before us. We see the royal rituals that surround a new birth in the household. The valorization of the birth of a son is discernible through the customs practised after his birth. The story also hints at the tradition of sending princes to Takkasilā to learn the Vedas. In the second part of the story we see the Bodhisatta successfully abolish the practice of animal sacrifice amongst his subjects. Thus, the negotiation and transformation of brāhmaṇical traditions is witnessed here. This seems ironical based on the passive presence of the queen mother and the juxtaposing of the local belief of worshipping a female spirit for offspring. As the story progresses, we see that during the Bodhisatta's reign not a single man was convicted for animal sacrifice. Thus, the Bodhisatta, without harming a single life, made them follow his teachings. This possibly hints at the diminished power of the tree goddess over the people's belief system, where animal sacrifice was so crucial.

A parallel to the royal tradition of sending their son away to study the Vedas can be traced to a brāhmaṇa's household in Takkasilā.[3] Here, a Bodhisatta was born as a brāhmaṇa in the city of Takkasilā. As he turned sixteen, he had two choices before him: he could either retire into the forest to pursue Brahmā and be a worshipper of the fire, or he could enjoy the life of a householder. He chose the joys of the household. Thus, his parents sent him to study under a renowned teacher. He paid the fees of a thousand pieces of money[4] to the teacher and returned, after completing his education. However, his parents now wanted him to forsake the worldly life and worship the fire. His mother wanted to make him aware of the wicked nature of women so she asked him to go back to his teacher and learn about the wickedness of women. The teacher asked the Bodhisatta to look after the former's mother and take care of her needs. The disciple followed all his master's instructions. This aroused a passion within the mother, and she wanted to be physically intimate with him. However, he refused her advances as she was his master's mother. She told the Bodhisatta that if he truly desired her, she would get her son killed. This made the Bodhisatta aware of the 'innate' sin of womankind. With this knowledge, the Bodhisatta forsook his worldly life. In this tale, although the mother had an equal role to the father in deciding the life of their son, the notion about the degraded nature of womankind has been generalized. The mother was keen to teach her son about the 'innate' nature of women. What becomes apparent is the negotiation of different attitudes in the Buddhist narratives: at one level, equal space was conceded to the woman in deciding the future of her son but on another level she also delivered to him a misogynist idea about the universal evil nature of women. This would suggest that ideally women were expected to internalize and communicate ideas about women's 'true' nature within the household.

Just like the story of the royal household here too the tradition of sending a son to Gandhara at the age of sixteen with the consent of both the parents becomes apparent. The parents in this narrative are also seen offering their son choices. But as the story progresses, the teacher's home at Takkasilā presents us with a different picture of the household. The teacher used to take care of his mother and would feed, clean and bathe her with his own hands. The deceptive nature of his mother was like a warning to the disciple, ultimately precluding him from embracing the life of a householder. In this narrative, while the mother is placed in a position of equality with the father in deciding the future of their son, the tone of the text, at the same time, stigmatizes the nature of woman. This is indicative of the complex nature of the Buddhist traditions.

The flamboyance of the royal household of Vesālī becomes evident in a story from the Jātakas where[5] the city's immense prosperity is marked by the triple boundary wall that protected the area. Inside the city were several kings ruling the kingdom. One of the princes in the royal household was very cruel and used to punish people ruthlessly. Because of this his parents brought him to the Buddha, who taught him the value of kindness. The active presence of the couple in mending their son's evil traits is notable. In the above story, the power play in the household is clear. The three-layered wall is indicative of the prosperity of the household, which required protection. The dependence of the royal couple on the Buddha, as well as the Buddha's active influence on the household, is also very significant. As in the examples discussed in previous chapters, the Buddha's intervention in restoring order within the household was crucial. Thus, the household was not visualized as a self-sufficient unit but as one dependent on the Buddha and the saṇgha.

Another variant of the above theme is found in the verse of *thera* Kuma's son.[6] From the commentary of this verse, we know that the *thera* was born to the family of a householder. We also learn the *thera* was named after his mother. After entering the Order he started living in the hills and corrected his mental exercises to attain arhantship. In his verse he spoke against the excess bodily needs exhibited by his fellowmen. He emphasised on right seeking and the right way of following the eight-fold path—'*Sādhu sutaṃ sādhu caritakaṃ sādhu sadā aniketavihāroatthapucchanaṃ padakkhiṇakammaṃ etaṃ sāmaññamakiñcanassā 'ti*.'[7] The matrilineal identity of the *thera* is worth noticing in the midst of a society that largely advocated patriarchy. This clearly indicates heterogeneity in society. The *thera*'s abhorrence towards passion indicates the clear division of the social life of the householder and the asocial world of the *bhikkhu*.

A significant feature of parenting a child by a widowed mother surfaces in the instance of *thera* Kassapa.[8] Kassapa was born in a brāhmaṇa's household and brought up by his widowed mother. Once he heard the Master preach during his visit to the Jeta grove. Through this he recognized the futility of worldly life. He asked for his mother's permission to renounce the world and was anxious to join the Master in his religious tour of the countryside. Following his mother's word to go where he would be free from ties, he entered the saṇgha and attained arhantship. This instance hints at the position of widows in the social realm. Here, the widowed mother had quite an eminent place in her household. While many of the previous instances indicated the passive position of the wife in the household, the example of this widowed mother reveals a different picture. Beyond the conventional mother figure pursuing a married life for her son, the widowed mother is keen on her son gaining true liberation.

A similar situation arises in the verse of *therī* Uppalavaṇṇā with her father deciding to send her away from worldly life.[9]

Uppalavaṇṇā donated gifts to the Order and achieved the chief place amongst the *bhikkhunīs*. In her next birth (as a daughter of a treasurer) she was known for her physical grace. As she grew up, kings and common folk from all over the land wanted to marry her. Her father found it impossible to satisfy everyone. Finding himself in a difficult position, he thought of inspiring his daughter to renounce the world. He took her to the *bhikkhunī* quarters and got her ordained. Here we see a lot of negotiation between different households. Interestingly, Uppalavaṇṇā's father chose to solve the problem of her marriage by sending her to the alternative household in society—the saṇgha.

The idea of a separate women's chamber in the king's household is seen in some stories from the Jātakas.[10] In one such narrative we come across the women's chamber of the royal household of the King of Kosala. His queens lamented that they never had the opportunity to go to the monastery at their will to meet the Great Buddha. They also described their existence in the palace as surviving in a box. However, together they told the king about their common wish. As the story went one, the king went to listen to the Buddha's teachings. There he encountered a learned layman. He asked the layman to come to the royal harem and teach his wives. However, the man turned down his request and said that a layman should never go teach in a king's harem—this was only the prerogative of the Brethren. So the king asked his wives to choose a person from among the disciples of the Buddha to teach them religion. The queens' unanimous choice was the Buddha's chief disciple, Ānanda. With the Buddha's permission, Ānanda would teach the queens in the harem. One day, the king discovered that one of his jewels was missing. He began to suspect everyone in the palace; even his wives were not spared. However, with Ānanda's advice the king got back his stolen jewel. Everyone in the royal household remained grateful to Ānanda. In this narrative the picture of the king's household brings up several questions before us. We see that certain rules prevailed in the women's quarter of the royal household. The queens had no right to visit the monastery. This leaves us to interrogate access to spaces in the Buddhist tradition. In another part of the story we see that a learned layman was not free to teach women in the harem. He said that this was only the prerogative of the Buddha's disciples. The juxtaposition of these situations is interesting in understanding the marginalized position of queens in the royal household. This is evident from the situation when the king, on losing his jewel, didn't hesitate to suspect his queens.

The royal household as the chief almoners has been hinted at in the commentary on the verse of *thera* Kuṇḍa-dhāna.[11] The *thera* was born to a brāhmaṇa's household and trained in the knowledge of the Vedas in his early years. Later in his youth, he heard the Master preach and joined the saṇgha. King Pasenadi became influenced by him and provided him with everything he needed so he did not have to go begging for alms. Later in the narrative, the lay disciple Subhaddā, the daughter of Anātha-piṇḍika, who invited the Master and the brethren to dine at her place. *Thera* Kuṇḍa-dhāna then revealed his power and attainments to her. He recited his verse, addressing the brethren about the severing of the five-fold bonds of worldly life.[12]

In this commentary three different households have been juxtaposed and the instances of negotiations between them are worth mentioning. First, a brāhmaṇa after being endowed with knowledge of the Vedic corpus joined the Buddhist path upon hearing the Master's preaching. Second, the king's household became his main support. The king wanted to provide him with all necessities so that he did not have to collect alms. Last, the daughter of an ordinary household was able to invite the Master and the brethren to her home. This stands in contrast to the stifling position of women in the royal household.

That the 'harem quarrel'[13] was a common feature of the royal household becomes evident in another story from the Jātakas.[14] The king and Queen Mallikā were engaged in a 'harem quarrel'. The king was so enraged with her that he ignored her existence. The queen met the Master at Jetavana and told him about the king's wrath. The Master intervened in order to make peace between them. The next day he went to the palace for alms and asked the king about the queen. The king gave the Master alms and told him that the queen was intoxicated with the pride of her position and had become very arrogant. The Master immediately made the king realize that it was his decision to bestow power on her; therefore, it would be wrong of him to blame her. The king agreed with the Master and lived happily with the queen.

The relationship of the royal household and the saṇgha becomes apparent here. When the royal couple had a serious tiff, the queen found the Master to be her last resort. Remarkably, the harem quarrel was solved with the intervention of the Master. On the other hand, the Master and the brethren were dependent on the alms of the royal household.

A similar instance of rivalry between queens in the royal household of King Brahmadatta surfaces in a narrative.[15] One of the king's consorts was barren in her earlier birth and she prayed that a goblin might devour the child of her co-queen. This queen was under the spell from a previous birth and turned into a goblin to eat children. Each time the queen gave birth to a child the goblin would devour it. As a result, the king decided to employ a guard to protect the queen once she became pregnant again. The goblin was unable to kill the child and thus a Bodhisatta was born to the queen. He grew up in the strict custody, living in an iron house. When he was sixteen years old, the king wanted to give him the responsibility of his kingdom. Accordingly, the city was decorated and the Bodhisatta came out of confinement for the first time. He marvelled at the splendour of his father's kingdom and wondered about his long confinement. He wondered if his captivity was somehow his fault. As a result, he was told the story of the goblin who was after him, and who had already killed his brothers. After his procession in the city was over, he entered the royal household. The king was amazed to see the physical beauty of his son. He asked his courtiers to adorn his son with jewels and sprinkle him with the water from three conches. However, the Bodhisatta told his father that he did not have any interest in worldly life and wanted to renounce it. The king was surprised and asked the prince for a reason. The Bodhisatta told him that he had realized that even if he got rid of the goblin, he could never escape the bondage of old age or death. He asked for his father's permission before embracing a life of asceticism. However, the king followed his son and left the worldly life as well. Here, several aspects about the royal household are evident in the above narrative. The conflict among co-wives is apparent from the barren queen being jealous and devouring the children of her co-queen. The iron confinement where the prince was raised is interesting. It is where he received his education and wisdom. While he was literally confined to an iron house, when released from the same he was no longer attracted to his riches of his father's kingdom. To him, the worldly life of the royal household appeared to be a confinement, which he was ready to renounce. Later, instead of becoming the future king, he decided to leave the confinement of the royal household for the life of asceticism.

The security of the queen in a king's household can be questioned in the light of a story from the *Dhajaviheṭha-Jātaka*.[16] In this narrative, a wizard corrupted the chief queen of King Brahmadatta with magic. Her handmaids witnessed this event. This matter was later brought to the king's knowledge. He immediately asked his men to find the wizard. They realized that the wizard remained in the guise of an ascetic during the day and misbehaved at night. On hearing this, the king asked his men to banish all ascetics and Brothers from his kingdom. However, Sakka was able to help the king break free from his heretical views, and endowed him with the wisdom to recognize true ascetics. The king then called back all true ascetics and Brothers to his kingdom. He also resumed the process of almsgiving. We have already read about the provision of a separate chamber for the queen in the royal household in previous narratives. Despite this, however, the security of the queen in such confinement was not always assured. She was corrupted by someone in the guise of an ascetic, who were trusted in the royal household.

Instances of brāhmaṇas claiming rights over women of the royal household feature in a story from the *Juṇha-Jātaka*.[17] Prince Juṇha of Benaras was made the king after he finished his education in Takkasilā. After becoming king he was reminded by a brāhmaṇa about the promise he made to him. Earlier in his life, the prince, overlooking the brāhmaṇa, accidentally broke his begging bowl and told him that he would compensate him after he became king. On hearing that he was made the king the brāhmaṇa came to the royal household. At first the king ignored him. The brāhmaṇa immediately told him that one should not ignore a brāhmaṇa standing in his way. However, the king could not remember his encounter with him. After reminding the king of their meeting the brāhmaṇa asked him for villages, wives, dancing girls and so on. In the story the bargain between a brāhmaṇa and the king is notable. The brāhmaṇa asked for wives and dancing girls. In light of the narratives discussed previously, this allows us to suggest that gender relations in the royal household developed around the nuptial ties and beyond it.

Household Structure Beyond Wedlock

While the marginalized position of married women in general can be traced to the conventional household, a completely different scenario is apparent in the household of women located beyond marital bonds—these range from the courtesan to widowed and unmarried women. The structure of their household is intriguing in the midst of a highly patriarchal and misogynist society. Thus, it is intriuging to see how gender relations have been embedded is such 'non-conventional' households.

The courtesan is categorized as the 'other woman' in the conceptual framework of the Buddhist textual traditions. This otherness is manifested in different aspects of her being. For instance, a matriarchal model of a household outside wedlock was common in the establishment of the courtesan.[18] Thus, we are presented with a different picture of the urban household in the courtesan's dwelling. She was the matriarch in her household and was not ready to give favours without the stipulated payment even to her regular clients. Besides, she had the authority to turn out the merchant from her household with force when her words failed to achieve their purpose.

The independent existence of a widowed woman features in the representation of a brāhmaṇa's lay household. In the verse of *therī* Candā[19] she said that in her worldly life she was a poor widow without children and could not afford food and clothing. It was after meeting *bhikkhunī* Paṭācārā and following her advice that she realized her life's highest goal and liberated herself from worldly bondings—'*sā ca maṃ anukampāya pabbājesi Paṭācārātato maṃ ovaditvāna paramatthe niyojayi.*'[20]

Repeated mentions of interdependence between the royal household and the Order emphasizes the latter's relevance in the social sphere. The instance of a single woman securing identity outside marriage features in the verse of *therī* Sakulā.[21] She was born to the royal household and was a dedicated lay follower of the Master. One day she became inspired by the Master's ordination of a *bhikkhunī* to the highest rank and thought to achieve the same for herself. In her next births she practised merit by making offerings to the monastery. In the following birth she also assisted the Master in the acceptance of the gift of the Jeta grove. Later, she became a believer and attained arhantship.'[22]

Another variant of the same story features in the verse of another *therī.*[23] In her previous birth she was a domestic maid but gained merit through alms-giving. Because of her charity, she was born to an affluent household of an eminent brāhmaṇa in Kosala. However, after listening to the Master's discourse, she decided to renounce her worldly life. Constant repetition of the alternative way of prosperous rebirths for *therīs* and the notable transition from an ordinary lay household to an affluent one and finally the renunciation of everything to join the Order as a viable alternative is significant here.

Thus, in the *Therīgāthā* a different portrayal of the structural relations within the household becomes visible.

Sharply contrasted to the narratives in the Jātakas,[24] we get a varied manifestation of upward social mobility in the *Therīgāthā*. In the verse of *therī* Uttamā,[25] the elite household of a landowner is represented. Uttamā was a domestic servant in the household of a landowner. She observed her master to be involved in religion and a frequent almsgiver to the Order. Accordingly, she practised the act of observing fasts and acquiring merit. This resulted in her birth in the next Buddha era to a treasurer's household. Due to her immense dedication to the realm of religion, she could attain arhantship. Here we see a different picture from the conventional understanding of marriage to a high-status man as the only means of changing status for a woman. In this commentary the *therī* Uttamā performed meritorious deeds to gain merits, which finally resulted in her rebirth in a wealthy family and the improvement in her status.

Almsgiving by the lay household to the saṇgha ranged from objects of regular use to groves and cells for residence. In the verse of *therī* Khemā[26] we are introduced to her various births in different households. In her first birth she was a slave and dependent on others for her livelihood. On seeing the Elder seeking alms, she gave him three sweet cakes and cut off her hair before handing it to him. As hair signifies female beauty, this perhaps is indicative of her disinterest in worldly desires. Across her different births, she continued giving alms to members of the saṇgha. After many fortunate rebirths, she became a queen of the royal household and continued her almsgiving activities. Now reborn in a wealthy family, she built a great park and donated it to the Order. In her next birth she donated a cell to the Order. She was then born as the queen of Bimbisāra and, becoming infatuated with herself, began to ignore her religion. This was brought to the notice of the Master, who made her realize her mistakes. At long last she joined the Order. Māra, the evil spirit had come across her path to tempt her; however, he could not succeed in derailing her.

Like the *Therīgāthā*, the verses of *bhikkhus* in the *Theragāthā* throw light on their move from home to homelessness. However, the transition in the lives of *bhikkhus* has been portrayed as a more naturalized process and has less-dramatic representations compared to its counterpart in the *Therīgāthā*. Yet, the verses narrating their renunciation present before us several variations regarding households.

Wealth, domesticity and renunciation occur in a pattern in the understanding of households. This becomes evident in the verse of *thera* Gosāla[27] who was born in a wealthy family of Magadha. After learning about the renunciation of a person of the same status, he thought to himself: if a person of that magnitude could renounce the world, he should follow him. Thus, he joined the Order and started dwelling in an upland area near his village. As he knew his mother regularly donated to *bhikkus*, he went to her for alms and was given porridge to eat. After eating and feeling refreshed, he gained insight of mind and attained a higher level of meditation.[28] In this commentary the transition in the notion of space is notable. Besides, the dependence of the *thera* on the household after renouncing the same is remarkable. Here the transition in bonding with one's worldly life is significant.

In this particular section the structural understanding of the household adds to our comprehension of gender relations in terms of marriage. It is evident that certain rituals such as the name-giving ceremony and sending children to educational institutions were specifically meant for sons. In many cases the husband had an important voice in decision-making regarding the child and the passive presence of the wife in this context is striking. However, the occasional presence of the wife as an equal partner and the widowed mother with an active voice in the household hint at the multifaceted attitudes depicted in the texts. Besides, the possibility of widowed women with independent existences in poor households has also been represented.

Contrary to the patriarchal household model, the courtesan surfaces as the sole matriarch of her establishment. This highlights her independent and powerful status, where she not only had the power to name any price for her company, but could also exercise discretion in donating to the saṇgha. The *Therīgāthā* also points to such important instances of almsgiving. In this particular activity, the striking presence of the woman as an almsgiver irrespective of her marital status is notable. A remarkable comparison with the Jātakas crops up when the *Therīgāthā* speaks about instances where women took decisions independent of learning the doctrine and donated to the saṇgha despite their matrimonial status. However, in the *Theragāthā*, the household features as a ground of sufferings. Marital relations and other worldly ties within the household have been described in the context of the *thera* severing this bond with them. What is evident then is that the household is represented as a gender-differentiated space in all three categories of texts, with different aspects highlighted based on the textual tradition in which the household is represented.

Relations of Dependence and Hierarchy within the Household and 'Beyond'

An understanding of nuptial ties would remain incomplete without discussing relations of hierarchy perpetuated through the factor of dependence in a wide range of households explored in the previous section as well as 'beyond' it. Although androcentrism and patriarchy were a part of Buddhism, there were historical attempts to challenge the conventional discriminatory attitudes and structure within this patriarchal social set-up. It becomes evident from the multifaceted narratives of the Buddhist texts that women's spaces within the household or the Buddhist saṇgha were neither fixed nor unalterable. There were several instances where women made their presence felt and found their niche, both in the household and the saṇgha. At other times they had to face resistance from the patriarchal society and succeeded in surmounting it.

The confrontations between two different kinds of households is represented in a narative from the *Dasaṇṇaka-Jātaka*,[29] specifically between the royal household and the household of the royal priest. The son of the royal priest came to meet the king. Seeing the queen, he became enamoured by her. On hearing his condition the king said that he would send the queen to the priest's house for seven days to stay with the priest's son. As the queen was taken to the priest's house, his son was delighted with her. They became enamoured with each other and fled to another kingdom. Instead of returning to the royal household on the eighth day, as dictated by the king, they absconded from the priest's household to an unknown place. Great sorrow befell the king and no physician could cure him. With the intervention of a Bodhisatta the king realized that it was not worthy of him to pine for the queen, who had never loved him. The interesting instance of a close interaction between royal and ordinary households is notable. Here, we could barely trace the queen's voice of consent in the royal household. She was sent by the king to the priest's house as the priest's son desired her. The silent presence of the queen is significant. However, we see that in the ordinary household she was treated well and became enamoured with the priest's son. Interestingly, she took the bold step of absconding with her companion out of fear of returning to her royal abode.

The queen as a significant adviser to the king in the royal household is relatively rare, yet an instance of this surfaces in a story[30] where we learn of the sixteen dreams of the king of Kosala. The brāhmaṇas of the royal household interpreted his dreams and predicted severe danger. They suggested the only solution was in expensive sacrifices and offerings. It is very clear that the brāhmaṇas planned to take advantage of this situation. Soon after, the queen Mallikā came to know about this. She immediately asked the king to meet the Master, who was the chief brāhmaṇa of this world and the world of the devas. The king acted as per the advice of the queen. He met the Master and described his sixteen dreams to him. The Master interpreted the king's every dream and also pointed to the effects the dreams could have in the distant future without harming the king. In this narrative, we get a clear idea of the interdependence of the royal household and the brāhmaṇas. Moreover, we also see that given an opportunity the brāhmaṇas would exploit the king to further their own interests. Here, the queen can also be seen as a benevolent adviser to the king in his hour of need. It was on her advice that the king met the Master, who gave him the ultimate solution and revealed the fraud of the brāhmaṇas of the royal household. The contrast between the brāhmaṇical tradition and the Buddhist monastery becomes apparent in this narrative.

In another instance the discretion of a queen was doubted by the king within the royal household. This narrative also emphasizes the relationship between the royal ladies and the

Order.[31] In the royal household of the king of Kosala, the Elder Ānanda used to preach to the ladies of the palace. The women made a gift of 500 robes to the Order. However, the king became suspicious as the Buddha allowed each monk to own only three robes and asked the monk about the robes. To this Ānanda said that he gave those robes to the Brothers in the saṇgha, whose clothes were worn out. Here the close connection between the royal household and the saṇgha is apparent. The Elder used to preach the dhamma to the royal ladies. In exchange he got a gift of robes that he sent to the monks who were in dire need of clothing. However, the king was sceptical about the decision of the queens and was not sure if they were donating judiciously to Ānanda. This also hints at three major points: one, the king did not trust his queen's discretion in donating to the Order; two, he was not well aware of Ānanda's noble qualities; and three, there must have previously been many miscreants who faked being *bhikkus* in order to fool members of the royal household and earn alms.

Another variation of this issue can be traced to a story[32] related to the household of a great merchant from Benaras. A Bodhisatta, born as the merchant, was very liberal and fond of almsgiving. He had alms halls built at the four gates of the city, in the middle of the city and at close proximity to his own house. The news of his almsgiving became so widespread that Sakka became insecure and thought of dethroning him. He started hiding all the wealth in the merchant's household so that he would finally stop the process of almsgiving. However, no crisis could stop the Bodhisatta. He always tried to find a feasible alternative to distribute his wealth to the destitute. He suggested to his wife that she should not cut off her charity under any kind of adversity. His wife said that there was nothing left in the house except the dresses they were wearing and hence almsgiving would not be possible. However, the Bodhisatta started mowing grass, selling it and continued with almsgiving. At the end of the story we see that Sakka recognized the genuine charity of the Bodhisatta and gave him back all his lost wealth. In this narrative, a picture of a wealthy merchant's household where almsgiving was a significant activity is evident. The lady of the house too had an equal role in their acts of charity. Even at the time of crisis we see the merchant did not hesitate to mow grass and earn money to donate alms. This narrative, thus, hints at the flexibility of changing professions in contemporary society.

What is important to notice in the context of gender relations in the Buddhist narratives is the power play within the royal household. The queen was often seen wielding her charm to further her own interests. This becomes clear in a story from the *Bandhanamokkha-Jātaka*.[33] The king asked his queen for any boon she wished. Interestingly, she asked him to abandon the company of other women. From then on, the king never looked at any women in his harem with love. On the contrary, the queen seduced the king's messengers in his absence. However, it was the Bodhisatta who proved to be problematic for the queen. Even in the face of the queen's threats, he refused to commit any sin. On the king's return the queen filled him with false stories, blaming the Bodhisatta for her actions. The king announced severe punishment for the Bodhisatta who happened to be one of his most trusted officials. The Bodhisatta told the king that he was a born brāhmaṇa and had never been dishonest in his life. He revealed the reality of the queen to Brahmadatta. He asked the king to forgive her and said that nothing could be done as women were born with innate wickedness.

In the above narrative we see the power the queen exercised. She could prevent the king from being intimate with any other women and was so independent that she was was involved in physical intimacy with the king's messengers. She exhibited an extreme level of her power by threatening the Bodhisatta's life.

Another instance of a manipulative queen features in a story[34] of the royal household of the great King Dasaratha of Benaras. Amongst his 16,000 wives the eldest bore him two sons and a daughter. The elder son was Rāma the wise, the younger son was Prince Lakkhaṇa and the daughter was known as the lady Sītā. In course of time their mother died and the king remarried. Prince Bharata was born to the new queen. The king told the queen to ask for any boon she desired. The queen immediately asked him to make Bharata the king after him. At this the king was very angry as he had two other sons who were rightful claimants to his throne. However, for twelve years the two princes along with their sister Sītā were exiled to the forest. After the death of the king, Bharata went to the forest to bring back his elder brothers and sister. He asked Rāma to assume his rightful place as king. However, Rāma sent a pair of straw footwear to rule the kingdom instead of him. After the completion of twelve years he went back to the kingdom and was made the king. Lady Sītā was made his queen consort.

In this narrative, the royal household is the central ground for a number of issues. The king was seen to have as many as 16,000 wives, hinting at the prevailing practice of polygamy in contemporary society. In the process of fulfilling the boon of one of his wives, he found himself in a dilemma. His children were forced to leave the security of the royal household, which was no longer a safe environment for them. This reveals the wicked nature of the queen, making the king more aware of the treacherous nature of women. As the story progresses, we also come across an instance of marriage between siblings, which was accepted by society. Thus, the gender relations constructed in this story are significant.

The gendered notion of hospitality as an important part of the household features in the narrative[35] of two different households: one was that of an ordinary man who gave shelter to a Bodhisatta, the king of Benaras, at the time of distress, and the second was the royal household. As the man took the king to his house, he made him sit on his own special seat. He asked his wife to bathe the king's feet with water. After that he arranged the best possible food for the king and made a bed for him to lay down. The royal horse was taken care of as well by the layman. As the king left, he told the man to visit his palace. When the layman visited the king's palace he received very cordial treatment from the king. The king asked his queen consort to wash his friend's feet and himself sprinkled water on him. The king accepted the gifts brought by the man and, later, gave him half of his kingdom. The marginalized position of women in both households is clear from this tale. Bathing the feet of a male guest seems to be a common gesture, whereas any such gesture with the genders reversed has never been mentioned in any of the Buddhist texts.

The son born to the chief queen had an important position in the law of inheritance. We get an idea of this in the royal household of King Janasandha.[36] A Bodhisatta was born as a son to the chief queen of the king. As he grew up his father made him learn the three Vedas and duties of the world. The king died during the seventh year of the prince. The courtiers performed the obsequies of the king with great pomp. On the seventh day, they gathered to decide who would rule as the prince was very young. However, they came to the decision that they would test the prince's wit and would then decide if he could be made their king. They tested the prince, who managed to outdo them with his wit and knowledge. Thereafter he was made the king and ruled very judiciously. What is visible in this story is the partial implication of primogeniture as the law of inheritance after the king's death. Although he was assigned to be the possible future king—being the son of the chief queen—the ultimate decision was taken by the ordinary people of the country before he was made the king.

The image of the king's household at times took an interesting turn due to the presence of mediators.[37] The king had a daughter who fell in love with his nephew. They were brought up together in the king's palace. Initially, the king thought of getting them married and making his nephew the future king. Later he thought that such a decision would not be beneficial for his worldly gains. So he decided to initiate a matrimonial alliance for his daughter with another royal household. In the meantime the king's nephew hired a wise woman to act as a mediator so he could escape with his lover. The woman told the king that his daughter was under the influence of witchcraft and needed to be treated urgently. The lovers made an escape successfully with her assistance. As the story ended, we see that the king accepted their marriage. His nephew was made the future king and his daughter his queen consort. In the above narrative, the picture presented of the royal household is quite unconventional. We get an idea about the unconventional role the brāhmaṇa played in the royal household. Besides, the practice of marriages between cousins was represented as a common practice. The idea of matrimonial alliances between two royal households and the expansion of territorial rights as a result of it is noteworthy. We also see that the territory was passed to the nephew of the king in the absence of his son. This is indicative of a variation in the conventional law of inheritance.

The narratives of the Jātakas unfold instances of conflict in the household. In one such story a young man took responsibility of his household after the death of his father and took good care of his mother.[38] It was after his marriage that his wife started complaining about the presence of his mother. The man asked his mother to leave their household and live elsewhere. Having no other option she left the household and worked for a living. After she took leave of her son's house a son was born to the couple. The man's wife told him that it was because she left that such fortunate incidents were taking place. On hearing this, the old woman was extremely sad and she prayed for justice. As the story ends, we see that her son realized his mistake and came to her for mercy.

The narrative makes it clear that the wife had a decisive voice in the household. She played an important role in influencing her husband against his own mother who depended on him. However, the old lady was independent and earned wages to support herself outside the household. On the contrary the son appears as a mere vulnerable individual, who could easily be manipulated. Yet, he realized his guilt and asked his mother to excuse his sins.

In a story from the *Gahapati-Jātaka* we come across a Bodhisatta, who was born as a householder's son. He married and settled down with a woman who was not loyal to him. She maintained an intimate relationship with the village headman in the absence of her husband. Once, during a bad harvest season the crops were damaged, causing a famine in the village.[39] All the villagers became indebted to the Bodhisatta. Thereby, taking advantage of the opportunity, the headman visited the Bodhisatta's house in his absence and enjoyed time with his wife. On returning, the Bodhisatta saw them together. He taught them a lesson by whacking them hard. Never did they dare see each other again. Here, the household is presented in an unconventional light. While it was the space the Bodhisatta shared with his wife, in his absence, the household became a space meant for the two lovers. However, the same space changed into a ground of contestation when the Bodhisatta caught his wife with her paramour.

A central feature of ascetic life was the rounds of begging for sustenance. In the process, ascetics had regular interaction with the lay household. This feature in Buddhist narratives suggests complex confrontations between the household and the Order. For instance, in one such story[40] we come across the lay household of a young man of Sāvatthī. After hearing the teachings of the Master he realized the impossibility of pursuing a holy life as a householder. Determined to embrace asceticism he gave all his wealth to his wife and children and went to the Master to be ordained. However, he used to return to his wife regularly for alms and food. One day his wife told him that a house has no meaning without a master, so she would leave the household as well. On hearing this he was confused; he decided to give up asceticism and return to his worldly life. In this narrative we see the dynamics in the life of a householder. A number of shifts in the household of the man are very evident. The interdependence between the lay household and the ascetics is interesting. On the one hand the man had to leave his household to be an ascetic, on the other hand he returned to his old life out of fear of losing his wife.

The general tone in the *Therīgāthā* hints at aversion to the life of a householder. Yet there are constant references to the *therīs*' households in their past lives. In the verse of a *therī*,[41] she has been addressed as Sumaṅgala's mother. Her son grew up to become an arhant. She became a *therī* after reflecting upon the miseries of her life as a householder. In this commentary, her identity as a mother in the worldly life does not cease after renouncing the same. What is remarkable is the fact that instead of being identified by her patrilineal descent or by her marital status, she was known by her son's identity.

Breaking ties of domesticity was common for the *theras*. Compared to the *therīs*, severing bonds with children do not feature as a cause of suffering for the *theras*. In the verse of *thera* Singāla-Pitar,[42] he was born to a wealthy household. After getting married a son was born to him. He named him Singāla and came to be known as Singāla's father. Later he renounced the life of a householder and learnt dhamma from the Master. Eventually he started living in the woods with his fellow *theras*. In the commentary the *thera*'s transition in the context of his dwelling is discussed. He moved from the secure life of the home to homelessness. He renounced his marriage and the son born within wedlock to attain arhantship.

The miseries of worldly life and the household as a site of contestation can be best understood in a narrative from the *Mayhaka-Jātaka*.[43] A Bodhisatta was born in a family that owned huge assets. After his parent's death, he took care of his brother and diligently performed the task of almsgiving. It was after the birth of his son that he realized the miseries of a householder's life. Handing over all his responsibilities, wealth, wife and son to his younger brother, he renounced worldly life. As the story progressed, we see that the younger brother killed the Bodhisatta's son. Not only did he kill his nephew but he also destroyed the alms chamber made by the Bodhisatta. The Bodhisatta came back from the Himalayas and asked his brother about his son's death. He understood that his brother was the murderer and the destroyer of everything good. He made him realize his sins and renew the process of almsgiving.

Here, the household became the site of contestation between two brothers. The elder brother, as the owner of his family wealth, supported his younger brother and engaged in almsgiving. When he renounced the worldly life this entire responsibility shifted to his brother. This included not only his children but even the right to the elder brother's children. The same household became a ground of contestation when the younger brother killed his nephew and stopped the tradition of almsgiving.

The transition from home to homelessness is associated with a wide range of alternative dwellings as explained in terms of 'beyond'. For instance, *thera* Tissa[44] used to dwell in a woodland settlement after renouncing his domestic life. The Master used to surveil the *thera* in the Order. In the dwelling, he was fast asleep with mouth wide open and the Master shed glory on him. Later he realized the futility of worldly passion and attained arhantship.

The image of worldly suffering in the lay household and its ultimate end in the Buddhist order is quite common in the *Therīgāthā*. The verse of *therī* Bhaddā of Kapilas[45] discusses her everyday bickering with her in-laws. Once, she was jealous of her sister-in-law giving alms to the Buddha. She dreaded the fact that the alms giving would end up earning merit for her sister-in-law. So she added mud into the Buddha's bowl. However, she later realized her mistake and filled the bowl with sweets. In her next birth, she was born with a foul-smelling body and donated all her gold to the Order to gain merit. Thus she was reborn to a wealthy household and became a beloved wife. In her very next birth she was born to the king's household. As a princess she lived a glorious life and attended on the Buddha diligently. Later she lost interest in worldly life and practised asceticism. Then she was reborn to a clan of Kosiya in a brāhmaṇa's household. She was reared in a very prosperous environment and was married to a suitable groom. However, she decided to renounce the world and handed over her wealth to her kin. She started dwelling in a grove for several years and eventually attained arhantship.

This commentary has developed through the portrayal of several rebirths of the *therī* through a range of households. We see that the royal household and the Order shared a mutual relation of dependence as almsgiving features as a revered activity for householders beyond the gender barrier. Parallel to this lay household, the constant emphasis on detachment from wealth is evident from the *therī*'s abandoning of wealth and her renouncing of the world.

The household as a shifting and changing idea could be seen in the story from the *Araṇṇa-Jātaka*.[46] Here we come across the household of a Bodhisatta born in a brāhmaṇa's household. The Bodhisatta went to Takkasilā for education. It was after the death of his wife that he adopted the religious life and went to the Himalayas. There he left his son in a hermitage and went to gather fruits. In the meantime a damsel fled to the hermitage for refuge and seduced the youth. She asked him to abscond with her, to which he did not agree. He said that he would wait for his father's return before leaving. On returning to the hermitage, his father understood his son's dilemma and helped him make a choice. As the story ends we see that the son decided to stay with his father and follow the righteous path.

In this narrative we come across a brāhmaṇa's household. Once again, the tradition of going to Takkasilā for education is emphasized. Interestingly, the continuous shift of the brāhmaṇa's household under changing circumstances is discernible: the brāhmaṇa went to Takkasilā as a teenager; he then shifted to the mountains with his son after his wife's death. We see that his son was left in the hermitage as he went to hunt. In the end, the dilemma of the son about leaving the hermitage speaks in favour of the lack of permanence attached to the idea of the household. The dependence of the brāhmaṇa on the Buddhist righteous path is a noteworthy aspect of this story.

Another variation of this can be seen in a story[47] of a *kuṭumbika* (a rich man who owned many estates. The involvement of animal characters in the narrative is significant. A Bodhisatta was born as an ox on the *kuṭumbika*'s estate. He had a little brother. Both of them did the draught work for the household. When the marriage of the *kuṭumbika*'s daughter was fixed with the son of an affluent household the *kuṭumbika* began to fatten a pig for the wedding guests. Seeing the pampering of the pig the younger ox felt jealous. He complained to his elder brother that inspite of doing all the draught work they were never fed like the pig. To this the brother explained to him that the pig was being fattened for the wedding feast. In the story, the animal characters represent the vulnerable individuals of the household. The powerful section always exploits the marginalized to meet their goals. Nonetheless, a relation of dependence often develops based on this hierarchy. This entire scenario developed in the backdrop of the wedding at a rich man's household where he reared an animal for the grand feast—which is symbolic of his affluence and power.

The insecurity of a domestic partner becomes quite visible in a story[48] relating to the household of an old *kuṭumbika*.[49] He married a young wife who bore him a son. He believed that as his wife was young, she would marry some unknown person after his death. So he decided to hide his treasure underground. He revealed this only to his household slave and asked him to tell his son this secret after he grew up. After the death of the *kuṭumbika* his wife asked the son to find the treasure and take care of the household. The slave, after some initial reluctance, helped him find the treasure. After finding the money he looked after his household and spent his life in charity and good work. Here the marginal in the household has been represented in a different paradigm and the power relation in the narrative operated in a unique way. The man was apprehensive of his wife's remarriage in his absence so he entrusted the slave with the secret of his wealth. He did not confront his wife about his insecurity; hence, the transfer of wealth has been dealt with very differently. In the narrative it becomes apparent that the *kuṭumbika* trusted his slave more than his own wife. He suspected her of trying to marry again after his death. To secure his son's future he hid his wealth. Even his slave showed some initial reluctance to reveal the location of his wealth. Following the advice of the Bodhisatta, who had been born as a friend of the *kutumbika*, the son recovered his father's wealth. He then took charge of his household and gave in charity and performed other good work.

Conclusion

Although the portrayal of the worldly household and its alternative model in the Buddhist saṇgha was widespread in all three texts mentioned here, the structural representations and variations in the portrayal of the household as a spatial idea reveals the difference across all three texts.

The household appears as a body that is united and structured by certain laws and rituals. This has been discussed above while referring to the three texts. We perceived the gendered nature of these norms as well. For instance, the birth of a *therī* brought immense poverty for her family, which stood in contrast to the birth of a *thera*, which was deemed to be a good omen for the family.

Apart from this, we see that in the *Therīgāthā* and the *Theragāthā* greater emphasis has been given on the almsgiving aspect of lay households to the saṇgha. In contrast to the Jātakas, marriage as the only way for the upward social mobility of women is absent in the *Therīgāthā*. Here, donative skills and meritorious deeds feature as the potent mechanism of climbing the rungs of the social ladder. Female members of the family are seen actively participating in almsgiving. Incidences of women seducing ascetics in the social sphere feature occasionally. Yet this does not stand in the way of monks going to women for alms. In fact, the act of almsgiving has been valorized to a great extent. I had intended to prise out information about the household as a site for several activities grounded on nuptial ties. The Buddhist textual traditions regarded the household as a centre of production, reproduction and consumption. The idea of a structural hierarchy and relations of interdependence within the household surfaced in varied layers. What becomes crucial is the fact that male and female identities had defined roles and responsibilities within the household. But these roles were not static and can be best understood in terms of specific socio-political contexts.

What one finds visible along with the hierarchical divisions within the household is the relation of dependence between the powerful and underprivileged. In the Jātakas, the understanding of matrimonial relations develops through heterogeneous possibilities. We come across instances of compatibility, infidelity, and unequal power relations arising out of the shared spaces within the household. This allows us to perceive gender bias at varied levels. For instance, the remarriage of the husband was considered a natural eventuality, but on the contrary even the thought of the wife remarrying after the husband's death made the husband insecure. Often, the donative interests of ordinary and lay couples were the reasons of their compatible marriage. Yet other possibilities were all pervasive. However, the *Therīgāthā* provides limited knowledge about the experience of married couples within the household. Endless bickering stemming out of marital ties or *bhikkhunīs* joining the Order as a means of ending worldly suffering are recurring themes in the verses. In the *Theragāthā*, the household has been represented as a mere obstacle that can be easily surmounted by a determined *thera* by joining the Order. Even the seductive advances of their wives failed to stop them from renouncing the bondage of worldly existence.

In the three texts dealt with here, worldly ties as the cause of every suffering is a common motif. Unlike the *Therīgāthā* and the *Theragāthā*, the Jātakas do not emphasize the renunciation of home as an individual's ultimate goal, whereas almsgiving beyond gender and class barriers remains one of the important concerns in the narratives. Overall, the Jātakas represent the household as a porous space, where entry was possible through marriage and birth. Members of different social categories could share the space on a short-term or a long-term basis. In contrast, the representation of the household in the *Therīgāthā* and *Theragāthā* is more monolithic. People escape from it to attain liberation. Individuals (both men and women) leave the household in the Jātakas as well, but for a variety of other reasons.

This provides us with a more complex understanding of the household.

NOTES

1. Tara Sheemar Malhan, *Plunging the Ocean: Courts, Castes and Courtesans in the Kathāsaritsāgara*, New Delhi: Primus, 2017, p. 43.
2. E.B. Cowell, ed., *The Jātakas*, New Delhi: Munshiram Manoharlal, 2002, *Dummedha-Jātaka*, story no. 50.
3. Cowell, *Asātamanta-Jātaka*, story no. 61.
4. The currency is usage at the time was Karshapana. However, in this narrative, only 'pieces of money' are mentioned.
5. Cowell, *Ekapaṇṇa-Jātaka*, story no. 149.
6. Rhys Davids, *Psalms of the Early Buddhists*, London: Pali Text Society and New York: Luzac and Co., 1964, canto 1, part 4, commentary XXXVI, verse 36.
7. H. Oldenberg and R. Pischel, *The Thera- and Theri-gatha (Stanzas Ascribed to Elders of the Buddhist Order of Recluses)* (online version), London: Pali Text Society, 1883, verse 36, see http://gretil.sub.uni-goettingen.de/gretil/2_pali/1_tipit/2_sut/5_khudd/theragou.htm, accessed 10 April 2016.
8. Davids, *Psalms of the Early Buddhists*, canto 1, part 9, commentary LXXXII, verse 82.
9. Ibid., canto 11, commentary LXIV, verse 224–35.
10. Cowell, *Mahāsāra-Jātaka*, story no. 92.
11. Davids, *Psalms of the Early Buddhists*, canto 1, part 2, commentary XV, verse 15.
12. See Oldenberg and Pischel, *Thera- and Theri-gatha*, http://gretil.sub.uni-goettingen.de/gretil/2_pali/1_tipit/2_sut/5_khudd/theragou.htm, verse 15.
13. Ibid.
14. Cowell, *Sujāta-Jātaka*, story no. 306.
15. Cowell, *Ayoghara-Jātaka*, story no. 510.
16. Cowell, *Dhajavihetha-Jātaka*, story no. 391.
17. Cowell, *Juṇha-Jātaka*, story no. 456.
18. Cowell, *Aṭṭhāna-Jātaka*, story no. 425. Discussed in detail in the previous chapter.

19. Davids, *Psalms of the Early Buddhists*, canto 5, commentary XLIX, verse 122–6.
20. See Charles Hallisey, tr., *Therīgāthā: Poems of the First Buddhist Women*, London: Murty Classical Library of India, 2015, verse 125.
21. Davids, *Psalms of the Early Buddhists*, canto 5, commentary XLIV, verse 97–101.
22. Hallisey, tr., *Therīgāthā*, p. 60, verse 100.
23. Davids, *Psalms of the Early Buddhists*, canto 3, commentary XXXI, verse 45–7.
24. Cowell, *Jātakas*, story no. 306.
25. Davids, *Psalms of the Early Buddhists*, canto 3, commentary XXX, verse 42–4.
26. Ibid., canto 6, commentary LII, verse 139–44.
27. Ibid., canto 1, part 3, commentary XXIII, verse 23.
28. Oldenberg and Pischel, *Thera- and Theri-gatha*, http://gretil.sub.uni-goettingen.de/gretil/2_pali/1_tipit/2_sut/5_khudd/theragou.htm.
29. Cowell, *Dasaṇṇaka-Jātaka*, story no. 401.
30. Cowell, *Mahāsupina-Jātaka*, story no. 77.
31. Cowell, *Guṇa-Jātaka*, story no. 157.
32. Cowell, *Visayha-Jātaka*, story no. 340.
33. Cowell, *Bandhanamokkha-Jātaka*, story no. 120. Discussed in detail in Ch. 2.
34. Cowell, *Dasaratha-Jātaka*, story no. 461.
35. Cowell, *Mahāassāroha-Jātaka*, story no. 302.
36. Cowell, *Gāmaṇi-Caṇḍa-Jātaka*, story no. 257.
37. Cowell, *Asilakkhaṇa-Jātaka*, story no. 126.
38. Cowell, *Kaccāni-Jātaka*, story no. 417.
39. Cowell, *Gahapati-Jātaka*, story no. 199.
40. Cowell, *Indriya-Jātaka*, story no. 423.
41. Davids, *Psalms of the Early Buddhists*, canto 2, commentary XXI, verse 23–4. Discussed in detail in Ch. 1.
42. Ibid., canto 1, part 2, commentary XVIII, verse 18.
43. Cowell, *Mayhaka-Jātaka*, story no. 390.
44. Davids, *Psalms of the Early Buddhists*, canto 1, part 4, commentary XXXIX, verse 39.
45. Ibid., canto 4, commentary XXXVII, verse 63–6.
46. Cowell, *Araṇṇa-Jātaka*, story no. 348.
47. Cowell, *Muṇika-Jātaka*, story no. 30.

48. Cowell, *Nanda-Jātaka*, story no. 39.
49. See V. Fausboll, ed., *The Jātakas Together with its Commentaries*, vol. 1, London: Trubner & Co., 1877–96, p. 224, story no. 39.

4

Representing the Tradition of Liberation

An Understanding of the 'Beyond'

THE EXPLORATION of nuptial ties in Buddhist textual traditions in this volume has been undertaken with the primary motive of describing the life of the householder. In the Buddhist tradition the idea of the householder and renouncer stood in opposition to each other. Time and again the root of all suffering has been connected to worldly attachments, which happen to be the nodal point of the householder's life. Buddhist ethics recognized the Buddha, dhamma and the saṇgha as the three jewels and the existence of the saṇgha monitored the notion of the Buddha and dhamma.[1] Given the social background of prosperity and the rapid economic growth in the sixth century BC, investing labour in production and reproduction was rational. However, the constant encouragement by Buddhism to renounce worldly ties to attain *nibbāna* seems dubious in the situation, as a renouncer neither participated in production nor reproduction. The complexity dissolves with the valorizing of the *gahapati* as the perfect householder; he was recognized as an efficient producer, reproducer and support of the saṇgha.[2]

The Buddhist textual evidence emphasizes the absolute division between the life of the householder and the recluse. In doing so the brahmanical tradition of *sannyāsa* attained only by brāhmaṇas as well as the presence of other heterodox sects have been vehemently opposed by the Buddhist tradition.[3] However, the path of renunciation prescribed by the Buddhists was complex. Admission to the Order was not always a choice equally available to all. Besides, the hindrances in the path of renunciation were no less than the material obstacles in worldly life. Here, an attempt has been made to deal with a body of literature of the 'heterodox' tradition that deals with renunciation from a Buddhist viewpoint. The intertextual variation withirl the Buddhist tradition opens the ground for a comparative study of the concerned texts. Within this complex context we will focus on certain broad issues: the consent of the individual in renouncing worldly life and hindrances in the path of the recluse.

The Consent of the Individual

In previous chapters we have seen different representations of marriage in the early Buddhist textual traditions. Two of the most important phenomena within this varied tradition are of consent and conflict and how they have been represented in the negotiation of matrimonial alliances. However, the Buddhist tradition portrays marriage and the entry of an individual to domesticity as a potent cause of misery. Thereby, abandonment of worldly ties has been described as a possible way of ending all causes of sufferings. Joining the Buddhist saṇgha was not only represented as a viable alternative to the householder's life but also the means to attain *nibbāna*.

Yet, 'one can distinguish several kinds of conflicts within the saṇgha'.[4] What is interesting are the similarities and contrasts between marriage and renunciation in the texts. One can see in earlier discussions in this volume how the consent of individuals in matrimonial alliances was irrelevant and marriage strictly depended on the decision of the parents in most instances.[5] Indeed, we come across other possibilities of eloping partners, but the narratives indicated this to be improper.[6] In this chapter, an attempt will be made to visualize the nature of renunciation that stood as an alternative to domestic life. How far the individual's consent was necessary in opting for the life of a recluse will be analysed.

'Choices' before the Renouncers

Denial of social obligations latent in the life of the householder was the primary reason for recluses opting out of social life. This was no less of an individual choice. However, there were several other contexts that made an individual opt to be ordained into the Buddhist order. Here, I will attempt a comparative analysis of different aspects of marriage and renunciation using the Jātakas, *Therīgāthā* and *Theragāthā*.

While discussing royal marriages in Chapter 1, it becomes evident that the king played an important role in selecting his bride. This came about either through an alliance between two warmongers or due to the king's strong desire for a lovely maiden.[7] An identical situation features in the case of his renouncing domestic life. The king took independent decisions in determining the ideal moment to break ties with worldly life. Such instances featured a number of times in the Buddhist texts. A reference to the king, ruling in the realm of Videha, features in a story from the *Makhādeva-Jātaka*.[8] The king of Videha decided that he would renounce worldly life when his hair turned grey. One day, his barber put a grey hair on his palm; the king immediately bestowed the sovereignty of his empire on his son and left the royal household. He told his son and his ministers that he was old enough and had his share of pleasure in his life. Thus, he considered this to be the prime moment for renouncing worldly existence. Even during his rebirth he was born a king and then gave up everything to become a hermit. Here, the king is the sole decision maker who did not need anybody's consent before leaving the world.

Another variation of the above narrative of renouncing worldly comforts and finding immense happiness in the Brotherhood features in a story where a Bodhisatta is seen renouncing his worldly comforts and becoming a recluse in the Himalayas.[9] He and his followers took shelter in the royal household. Later the king of Benaras asked the Master to stay in his mansion as he was too old to travel. Eventually, the oldest disciple of the Master came to meet him. The king learnt from the Bodhisatta that his disciple was once a king and lived in splendour. However, he found happiness only after breaking his worldly ties and joining the Brotherhood. Appeased by this insight, the king returned to his palace, where the Master continued live.

Similarly, it is evident that the choice to renounce social life was solely the king's.[10] He was the universal monarch and possessed every precious thing imaginable in his worldly life. However, nothing could stop him from renouncing and embracing the path of asceticism. Ultimately, he mounted his horse and left the world in search of liberation and required nobody's permission to do so. He tormented himself with austerities to attain true knowledge. This once again speaks in favour of the ultimate decision taken by the king in choosing the life of an ascetic. Notably, he did not need to wait for anyone's consent.

Another instance of a determined king taking an independent decision in opting for the life of an ascetic features in the Master's great renunciation.[11] Here the Master describes his experience of renouncing the worldly pleasure of a royal life. He referred to a certain point in time when his wisdom was yet to mature. Thus, he left his kingdom in the quest for liberation. In the above examples even the king who is symbolic of universal power and all worldly pleasures renounces material wealth and the ties of a householder's life to embrace the Buddhist path of ultimate liberation. In these examples, the ease with which royal splendour could be surmounted was exemplary. The kings' respectice choices in entering domestic life were as independent as their ultimate decision to renounce the same.

Apart from instances of kings taking independent decisions to renounce the world, the scenario of other members of noble families are worth mentioning. A different attitude is explicated in the instance of the daughter of a wealthy merchant who made up her mind to join the Order.[12] She had no attachment to worldly and temporal things and wanted to attain arhantship from a very tender age. Her parents were strictly against it and prevented her from taking the vows as she was their only child. It was only after her marriage and after she had fulfilled her role as a devoted wife that her husband took her to join the Order. There she was revealed to be expecting a child. After a son was born to her he was reared in the king's household and later joined the saṇgha. As opposed to the king, who could make his own decisions without interference, renouncing worldly life was not an easy option for women, even those from an elite background. Similar situations can also be seen in case of women selecting their spouses in the royal household. In rare instances resolute women from elite households could select their partners.[13] However, they either had to elope with their paramours or they are represented as making the wrong choice in selecting their grooms. In the case of renunciation, though they had to overcome various obstacles to execute their choice, they could still be successful in their mission to enter the order.

The commentaries of the *Therīgāthā* also refer to varied situations in which the *therīs* abandoned their domestic lives. In a reference to the verse of a *therī*[14] whose name is not known we hear of her several rebirths.[15] In each of these instances her inclination towards the path of religion can clearly be assumed. She was reborn each time by the dint of her meritorious actions towards the faith. In one of her births she was married to a man of reputed background. Soon after, she heard the Elder Great Pajāpatī preaching the doctrine and became so influenced by this that she wished to leave the world. Inspite of her husband's initial disapproval, she convinced him to heed her wish to leave the householder's life. She made him understand her inability to lead a domestic life. Her husband ultimately took the *therī* to have her admitted to the Order.[16] With the consent of her husband the reverend sister ordained her and, later, the Master taught her the path of religion. Here the consent of the *therī*'s husband was significant before her entry to the Order.

Therīs capable of exercising their choice to join the Order were rare but not absent. This is true in the case of *therī* Jentī,[17] who was born into a royal family. On hearing the Master preach dhamma she attained arhantship. She reflected on the change that came over her and renounced the world. Here she is depicted as relatively free and the prior necessity of consent by her patriarchal lords has not been emphasized.

Comparing the above three instances it can be deduced that renouncing worldly life was easier for an unmarried woman than for one in wedlock. A married woman had to overcome a lot of challenges before joining the Order. However, as discussed earlier for the *theras* this was presented as a natural and less dramatic process. This is relevant even in the present century where gender still remains one of the primary dividing principles in society.

As we turn to the *Theragāthā* we come across parallel situations to the ones previously discussed. For instance, *thera* Piyaṇjaha[18] was born to a noble family amongst the Licchavīs. As he grew up he was reputed to be an unconquered fighter. He was well known for sacrificing even what was dear to him. Thus his name became synonymous with 'love renouncer'. On meeting the Master, he was influenced by his preaching and developed insight into his life. He started dwelling in the forest and realized the difference between worldly success and liberation. He said that he no longer found pleasure in narrowness of mind and preferred to dwell in solitude. Here too we do not see any emphasis on the prior requirement of consent from the elders of his family. He simply exited worldly life by following the Master's teachings. Thus, the independent decision of the recluse clearly features here. One can also observe the Buddha's preaching against sensual pleasure in a householder's life in the story of *thera* Rakkhita.[19] Rakkhita was born to a family of Sākiyan nobles and was one of the young men given by the Sākiyan and Koliyan rājās as escorts to the Buddha. The Buddha's teachings from the *Kunāla-Jātaka* converted them and they were taught lessons against sensuality. The *thera*, connecting the lesson with his insight renounced the world and attained arhantship.

Similiarly, *thera* Vitasoka[20] was also born to a royal household as the king's brother. As a lay disciple of *thera* Giridatta he became well versed in the Tripiṭakas. After seeing a grey hair on his head he realized the impermanence of physical traits. From then onwards he started practising insight and later took orders under *thera* Giridatta. Here, like the stories of kings discused previously, he also decided for himself the ideal moment of renouncing worldly existence and did not wait for anybody's consent.[21]

In contrast to the above situations, there are also other, varied understandings of severing bonds with worldly life in the early Buddhist texts.[22] In one such instance, a *kuṭumbika* of Sāvatthī (Sāvatthivāsī)[23] joined the Order. Before joining, he made arrangements for some luxuries. He made a hut and a storeroom to store necessary items and even asked his servants to cook for him. His constant nexus with worldly life is clearly manifested in these details. Giving in to all the comforts of mundane existence, he dwelt at the outskirts of the monastery. Once a number of brethren came across his chamber and were taken aback on seeing that he had amassed so many luxuries. They took him to the Buddha who enlightened him on the principles of simple existence. The *kuṭumbika* was ashamed and he chose to lead his life like his other brethren. From this we get the idea that the Master guided the *bhikkhus* who, at times, were derailed by worldly attractions. This narrative captures the varied possibilities of ascetic life. Here, the *kutumbika* was influenced by the ascetics and wanted to renounce his worldly life. Despite isolating himself, he could not refrain from the luxuries of social life. It was only after being enlightened by the Buddha's discourse that he was finally able to renounce worldly pleasures.

From the evidence gleaned from all three Buddhist texts, we are presented with multiple instances of individuals opting out of the comfortable space of the elite household. In cases where a recluse pined for the luxury of his past life, he was shown the right way by the Master. The choices made by the recluse in each instance were governed by their particular situations. In the popular portrayal of the Jātakas, the quest for liberation from worldly ties is as an important influencing factor in a person choosing the life of an ascetic. However, in the *Theragāthā* the insight gained by the *bhikkhus* and the realization of the impermanence of social life plays a pivotal role in *theras* joining the saṇgha. In case of the *Therīgāthā*, disdain for worldly life becomes clear in the texts and instance of exercising choices through diverse situations is indicated. What is notable is that generally a recluse of noble birth was successful in taking an independent decision in renouncing worldly life. He did not have to wait for the consent of his parents or elder members of the family. This can be compared to matrimonial alliances where examples of members of elite households other than the king selecting their partners in conjugal life were rare. Whenever such instances occurred it was looked down upon as improper. However, in the case of women of noble families they had to win the consent of their patriarchal lords before marriage as well as to renounce the world.

What is notable is that the Jātakas rarely represent women from higher status as renouncing the world. Thus, the gender differentiation vis-à-vis renunciation by such women seems more marked when we compare the Jātakas with the *Therīgāthā*.

Consent of the Elder Members of the Family

There are other instances where, in the case of common folk, the consent of the parents or other elderly members of the family before choosing the path of religion was an important condition in all the three texts. This presents before us comparable contexts of matrimonial alliances where the parents played a decisive role in negotiating marriages (discussed in previous chapters).[24] This is clear in the following cases.

Taking permission from one's parents before joining the saṇgha had far-reaching implications that at times went beyond the given gender norms. The disregard of worldly life by women was a common reason for their choosing the alternative establishment of the Buddhist saṇgha.[25] In one such case, a young daughter of the servant of the Master's disciple was married to a family of equal status but her husband did not support the faith. She remained indifferent to the disrespect bestowed on her. She remained a dedicated follower of the Buddha and made generous contributions to the Buddha's disciple. Realizing her husband's disinterest in her she decided to renounce the household and concentrate on her faith. With her parents' permission she joined the Order. Unlike the case of other matrimonial alliances, here the parents appear more lenient in approving their daughter's choice. Besides, her decision was not condemned as improper. Ultimately she was able to rid herself of her disrespectful married life.

An example of accommodating differences in the Buddhist tradition is evident in the instance of *therī* Sīhā.[26] With the passage of time Sīhā became more inclined towards her faith. On hearing the Master preach, she became a believer in the Buddhist faith and, with the consent of her parents, she entered the Order. But as she endeavoured to gain insight, she faced immense obstacles. She failed to tame her mind against the external charm of the material world. However, with the passage of time she gained wisdom and finally won arhantship. In her verse she narrates her tedious tryst with sensual desires. She speaks about being distracted by the desire of intercourse, which always disturbed her thoughts and left her with no peace of mind—'*ayoniso manasikārā kāmarāgena aṭṭitā ahosiṃ uddhaṭā pubbe citte avasavattinī. pariyuṭṭhitā kilesehi sukhasaññānuvattinī samaṃ cittassa na labhiṃ rāgacittavasānugā.*'[27] Here we see that despite her inclination to the faith and her entering the Order with the consent of her parents she faced obstructions in the path of religion because of her strong desire for sensual pleasure. This stands in contrast to the Jātaka narratives where marriages with the consent of parents were relatively successful and were marked by the passive presence of the daughters.[28]

In the verse of *therī* Sundarī[29] we are also told the story of her father, who was overwhelmed by grief at the death of his young son. On meeting *therī* Vāsiṭṭhī he realized the futility of worldly attachments. No sooner did he meet the Master than he got ordained to the Buddhist faith. On hearing this, his only daughter decided to follow her father and renounce the world. Her mother tried to stop her as she was the only heir to the family's wealth but such an obstacle could hardly stop her from fulfilling her heart's desire. Later, with the consent of her mother she renounced the world and gained a great following of *bhikkhunīs*. With the passage of time her mother and her attendants too followed Sundarī's path of renunciation. In the above narrative a *therī* influencing a layman with her teachings is significant. The daughter of the man then made a choice to renounce all her wealth and follow in her father's footsteps. Her religious inclination was favourable for her attaining arhantship. Initially, her mother was reluctant to let her join the Order but eventually she joined the saṇgha along with her attendants. Here, the factor of choice visibly operated in each instance, in turn influencing the other. The *bhikkhunī*'s determination and quality of leadership stands in contrast to the passive presence of daughters in many of the Jātaka narratives where the latter were merely considered their father's assets.[30]

As in the case of the woman recluse, the consent of parents was indispensible in the instance of her male counterpart. This has been hinted at in the story[31] of the son of a merchant of Sāvatthī. The merchant's son was influenced by a crowd going to Jetavana to meet the Master. Gradually he became interested in religion and wanted to join the Order. However, he was not able to be ordained without the consent of his parents. After some initial disagreement he managed to get permission from his parents and could enter the path of religion.

Besides obtaining permission from one's parents before renouncing the world, the approval of the king was also necessary at times.[32] A brāhmaṇa who was known for his goodness was patronized by the king of Kosala and given the highest position among all other brāhmaṇas. Once, he decided to try and test his own goodness. He wanted to know if the king valued his character or his lineage. He began to take coins from the royal treasury and was eventually caught. The king punished him like all other criminals. Th brāhmaṇa then revealed the reality of the situation and what he aimed to do. He asked the king to grant him leave so that he could renounce the world and join the Order. This is markedly similar to the story where the king approved the desire of his trusted brāhmaṇa to take his chief queen in one of the Jātaka narratives discussed in a previous chapter.[33] While the queen convinced the brāhmaṇa about his mistake, in this case the brāhmaṇa successfully followed the path of the Buddhist faith with the king's approval.

In another story *thera* Bhadda[34] was taken to the Order by his parents. For a long time his parents had remained childless and with the grace of the Master a son was born to them. When the child turned 7 they took him to the Master to ordain him under *thera* Ānanda. The boy entered the Order, was trained and remained on the right path. He was knowlegable enough to be ordained by the Buddha soon after. This narratives stands in contrast to the instance of the mother from a Jātaka narrative who lamented the fact that her son had joined the Order. She even hired a prostitute to seduce him back to the worldly life and agreed to arrange a marriage between them as a price.[35]

Another example of a mother permitting her son to join the Order is evident in the story of *thera* Adhimutta.[36] He left the world under the training of his uncle *thera* Sankicca and attained arhantship at a very young age. Thus, he went to his mother to seek permission for full ordination. On the way he was attacked by some men who wanted to sacrifice him to their deity. *Thera* Bhadda did not try to escape and explained to them how he was indifferent to any physical loss which was so impermanent. On hearing him speak, the robbers became so influenced that they too wanted to renounce the world and join the Buddhist order.

At the age of 7, *thera* Dabba, who was a child prodigy,[37] was highly attracted to the Buddha and thought of renouncing the world. He asked for his grandmother's consent for the same as she was his only guardian. She took him to the Master and he was accepted into the Order. By his own merit he practised meditation and the Master acknowledged his extraordinary skills. However, some other *bhikkhus* tried to ruin him out of jealousy and were condemned by the Order. Out of his virtuous compassion for others, Dabba excused them. Such instances allow us to believe that besides mothers who were overenthusiastic about the marriage of their sons (as discussed in an earlier chapter), cases of mothers permitting the renunciation of their only child were not rare. All the above examples explain how seniors in the family played a significant role in an individual's admission to the Buddhist order. This parallels instances of matrimonial alliance where parents chose partners to further their children's entry to the life of a householder.

The Role of the Master

Just as the concept of choice operated at varied levels and in specific situations, the Master played an inspiring role in drawing householders to the world of religion. This is similar to the narratives in Buddhist texts where the Buddha influenced confused fathers to select suitable grooms for their daughters.[38] The typical questions that arise out of this might be elucidated through the following examples. In the narrative of Losaka Tissa[39] we learn about his ill luck right from the moment of his birth. Everyone including his mother left him even when he was a toddler. He survived on the leftovers of others. Once, *thera* Sāriputta met him and felt pity for him. He asked if he would like to join the Brotherhood. To this Losaka agreed, but destiny did not cease to be cruel to him even he joined the Order. He never received alms to meet his needs. It was Sāriputta who fed him on the day he was supposed to pass away. Often the brethren in the saṇgha enquired about his ill luck and entry into the Brotherhood. To this the Master said that despite all his misfortune he was sincere in his faith and thus attained arhantship. Here we see the active role of the Master in rescuing an unfortunate person. A parallel instance can be seen in the failed marriage of a brāhmaṇa in one of the Jātaka narratives, who was was cheated by his unfaithful wife. The Master came to his rescue by suggesting that he thrash his wife to show her the 'right' way.[40] Violence against women as an excuse to tame them reflects the severe patriarchal approach of the Buddhist texts. This approcah glorifies masculinity and the act of inflicting physical violence on women.

Similarly, admission into the Buddhist faith based on the Master' choice is seen in the story of a landowner of Sāvatthī who suffered after of the death of his beloved son. [41] He turned into a living corpse and was plagued with immense grief. However the Master realized his potential to embrace religion. Accordingly, he went to meet the landowner and explained to him the futility of crying over worldly attachments.

Turning to the *Therīgāthā*, we come across the story of *therī* Sāmā[42] who hailed from a reputed family. After the demise of her dear friend she left her worldly life, but grief for her dead friend engulfed her and she could not concentrate on gaining wisdom. At last after listening to the Elder Ānanda preach, she gained true insight. These two instances can be compared to the woman who followed the instructions of her husband and did not weep at the demise of her son.[43]

The influence of the Master is seen in the admission of *thera* Ajita,[44] a follower of Bāvarī (a learned brāhmaṇa), to the Buddhist order. He was sent by his teacher along with two other disciples to the Master. Incidentally, Ajita was so satisfied by the Master's replies to his questions that he chose to enter the Order. Soon after he developed insight and attained arhantship.

At times the strong influence of the Buddha in leading individuals from home to homelessness was a tremendous success and was duly awarded by the king. This is seen in the case of *thera* Bandhura.[45] Bandhura became so influenced by the Master's preaching that he left his worldly existence. It did not take him long to attain arhantship. Then he went to the king and preached the Buddhist ethos and the four noble truths before him. The king became so influenced by his preaching that he built a great vihāra in the town and bestowed it to the *thera* with great honour. *Thera* Bandhura offered everything to the Order and continued on his rounds, collecting alms. This stands in contrast to the instance where King Pasendi became so influenced by the Buddhist religion that he provided a *thera* with all the necessities so that he did not have to beg for alms.[46]

Thera Mātaṅga[47] chose the path of religion out of a strange circumstance. He was rebuked by all for his idle nature. However, after being acquainted with the *bhikkhus* and hearing the Master preach the norms he became very influenced by the faith and entered the Order. He aspired to perform all the exercises undertaken by the *theras* and eventually overcame his own slothfulness. Here we see the role of the Master as a strong influence on a lazy person. Mātaṅga was influenced to the extent that he entered the saṇgha and became an active *thera*.

At times Brothers could be seen regretting their admission to the Order. A Brother once admitted to the Master that he was full of regrets for renouncing worldly life and joining the Order.[48] He said that he was enamoured by the charm of a woman and had lost all interest in religion. To this the Master answered that desire was like honey sprinkled over deadly poison. Both bring about the fatal end of anyone who consumes them. Thus, he could make the *bhikkhu* see reality. Here the Master is seen playing the same role in the case where he reunited the estranged couple by guiding them to the 'right' path, although the path in this case was entirely different.[49]

A similar instance of disobedient Brothers in the Order is also found in the case of a Brother who, after joining the Order, was admonished for his conduct by the brethren.[50] He was repeatedly told about the right path by his Brothers;

however, he never listened to them. Later, the Master made him realize his fault. This can be compared to the instance of the brāhmaṇa who left his adulterous wife and married again. He admonished his unfaithful wife but never lived with her again.[51]

Brothers returning to the worldly life after being unable to live the life of a recluse were not rare.[52] One such adherent of the Buddha not only left the saṇgha for worldly life but spoke ill of the Buddha and his doctrine. The Buddha later came to know about it from Sāriputta and explained to him the folly of the Brother. This can be compared to the instances discussed earlier where mothers forcing their sons into marriage were not successful. Whereas the *thera* ultimately broke the shackles of his married life, cases of forceful renunciation hardly ended in failure and the Master generally succeeded in bringing these men back to the right path. Through this I am trying to emphasize the fact that like forced marriages which later broke up, a parallel can be found in the narrative of this *bhikkhu* who entered the Order and, coming under vile influences, began defaming the Buddha and broke all ties with the Order.

Another incident makes the gendered nature of entry to the Order very clear. In this narrative we see that female lay disciples used to visit the Master in the daytime to hear him preach. Gradually, with the preaching schedule being moved to the later part of the day, women could no longer join this practice. This was probably because outings at late hours were not allowed for women. This then became an obstacle to them in their path of religion. Joining the Order was not free from inbuilt hindrances to male *theras* as well. This becomes evident in the instance of Elder Rāhula.[53] Rāhula's heart was set on attaining arhantship and, like a dedicated disciple, he went to the monastery at Kosambī after joining the Order. Yet, he was refused lodging with the Brothers as he only was a novice. They said that the Master preached against the cohabiting of Brothers and novices as it was a *Pācittiya* offence to do so.[54] Earlier, male disciples used to sleep in the service hall of the monastery. Once some disturbances were reported to the Master and he asked the brother to avoid the company of novices while sleeping. So when Rāhula came to the Order, they refused to give him lodging and asked him to seek his own shelter. At last, this was brought to the notice of the Master. He rebuked the Brothers and asked them to be lenient with the novices. In the previous part of thise narrative, gender-based restrictions in the Order are apparent. This indirectly hints at the possible obstacles and unequal social space for women. Besides the gender-based issues, Rāhula is seen facing hurdles regarding his basic needs in the monastery. As the story ended, we see that the Master intervened and solved his problem but the hindrance faced by female disciples remained unaddressed. Here, the gendered nature of the Order is very visible. This runs parallel to innumerable instances in nuptial ties that were markedly partial to the convenience of men.

All the above cases are indicative of the Master's influential role in an individual's choice of renouncing worldly life. This can be compared to the role played by the Master in matrimonial alliances. He not only assisted confused fathers in negotiating suitable alliances for their daughters, but also intervened in preventing marriage with deceptive partners. Also noteworthy is that the Master's influence transcended social divisions of gender and status.

Broader Social Ethics

A few factors like age, physical appearance and, most significantly, status played a significant role in negotiating matrimonial alliances, whereas the path to the Buddhist order was open to all irrespective of class, caste and age barriers. This will become clear through the following instances. Besides the presence of young Brothers in the saṇgha, joining the Order in one's old age was not rare. This becomes evident in a story from the *Māluta-Jātaka* where two men decided to join the Order in their old age.[55] Both of them had queries relating to changes in nature at the onset of the cold season. Despite pondering over the same for a long time, they could not come up with an answer. Thus, they went to the saṇgha to have the riddle solved by the Master, after which they ended up joining the Order, even in their advanced age. Age is supposed to be a factor in matrimonial alliances but the same was not implied in admission to the Order. The instance of *thera* Rādha[56] also proves that age was not a bar for entering the Buddhist order. He was born to a brāhmaṇa's household and in his old age was unable to perform his duties. He met the Master and conveyed his condition to him. With the consent of Master Sāriputta, he was admitted to the Order. Soon after he won arhantship and became very well versed in the Master's teachings.

Entry to the order at a mature age is reflected in the instance of *thera* Gotama.[57] He was born to a brāhmaṇa's household. In his youth he fell in bad company and lost all his money to a courtesan, leaving him destitute. Then he met the Master, who enlightened him taught him the right path. Eventually he entered the Order and attained arhantship. This was indicative of the all-inclusive nature of the saṇgha. Once, a lay companion asked him a question concerning wealth to which the *thera* explained in his verse that a person, to protect his earned wealth, should abstain from keeping the company of women. He had realized this truth through his own life experience. He also compared the use of insight over lust to the use of a knife in war and the ultimate journey to happiness in liberation.[58]

Women joining the Order was not rare; there are instances where elders among the bretheren are observed ordaining women.[59] In one such case an old woman brought the Elder Sāriputta to her house and took care of him. The king and all the other prosperous lay disciples sent alms to the lady so that she could take good care of the Elder. However Sāriputta only took things given to him by the lady. He enlightened her and converted her to the faith. This stresses the entry to the householder's life as more time bound compared to that of renunciation, which was open to people of every age.

In another story a Brother completely dedicated towards religion found it difficult to remain a householder. He renounced his family life and became an ascetic. Being the youngest amongst the brethren he received little importance and minimum share of alms. So he went to the wife he had abandoned. She filled his bowl and displayed respect towards him, and he was entirely captivated by her charm. His wife took advantage of this and played tricks to entrap him and bring him back to the worldly life. At last the Brother decided to return back to worldly life. However, the brethren took him to the Master and he came to know about his past birth where staying with his wife was harmful for him. The above narrative brings forth a lot of issues. From it, we learn about the hierarchy among the brethren. Besides, the constant transition in the mind of the Brother is notable. He was determined enough to leave behind his children and wife to join the Order but could not accept the neglect by the seniors in the saṇgha. In his vulnerable state of mind he could not overcome his wife's charms and decided to return to the life of a householder. It was through the Master's intervention that he realized his folly. The constant accommodation of diverse possibilities in the Buddhist tradition hints at the openness of the saṇgha which stood in sharp contrast to the limited nature of a householder's life.

That the saṇgha stood above any social barrier and could include all was attested by the entry of robbers into the Order. They were often considered reformed at the end, whereas their marriages were often portrayed as unsuccessful.[60] An interesting instance of the conversion of a blood-stained robber into an ascetic is traced to a narrative from the Jātakas.[61] Once, a robber named Aṅgulimāla saved the life of a pregnant woman. This incident played a transformative role in his life. As he gained merit from helping another, from then onwards he was able to accumulate food and other requirements with ease. Gradually he transformed into an ascetic and was recognized as one of the great Elders. Thus, this story is exemplary among the brethren as it shows that the teachings of the Buddha could lead to miracles. Without any kind of strict measures a cruel robber could be transformed into a renowned ascetic.

In many of the instances of the Jātakas, courtesans are seen desiring married life, but these repeatedly end in failure.[62] However, their entry into the Order was uninterrupted. As we turn to the *Therīgāthā*, we learn about the rebirth of *therī* Aḍḍhakāsī[63] as a prostitute because of her previous misconduct. In her earlier birth she chose the life of a *bhikkhunī* and was established in the Order. Once she reviled an elder sister by calling her a prostitute. It is assumed in the commentary that due to such misdeeds she was born as a prostitute. As a courtesan, she desired to leave the worldly life and wished to be ordained in the Buddhist faith. Her way was obstructed by the libertines of Benaras. However, the Master permitted her admission to faith. Then she worked on her insight and obtained arhantship. We see in the above narrative that the profession of a prostitute was looked down upon, so much so that it was assumed to be offensive if falsely implied for a woman and the punishment for this could be severe. Here, the *therī* born of a wealthy household became a prostitute due to her previous sins; thus, she decided to enter the path of religion. We have seen how this was met with overwhelming obstacles. Yet, with the Master's intervention she was able to join the Order and eventually became an arhant.

That joining the saṇgha was open to all across gender barriers is emphasized in the following instances. *Therī* Cittā[64] was born as a fairy. Worshipping the Buddha with flowers she gained merits and after several rebirths was born into a wealthy family. At a certain age she heard the Master preach and became inclined towards religion. As she grew older, she practised all the exercises of a recluse and gained enough insight to attain arhantship. This stands in contrast to the rags-to-riches stories of women in the Jātakas whose upward social mobility could be realized only through nuptial ties.[65] In the *Therīgāthā* the unique instance of alternative mechanisms of upward social mobility for women through almsgiving is recognized.

Other possibilities of renouncing the worldly life and entering the Order feature in the case of *therī* Mittā,[66] who gained merit by giving alms to a *bhikkhunī*. Due to her merits she was reborn into a royal family and was attracted to the Buddhist faith. Later, she left the world with Great Pajāpatī Gotamī. After her training she finally attained arhantship. In her verse she expressed the hardships she underwent to detatch herself from worldly ties. She ate one meal, shaved her head, wore the robe of a nun and thus could overcome all her worldly dilemmas—'*sājja ekena bhattena muṇḍā saṃghāṭipārutādevakāyaṃ na patthe 'haṃ vineyya hadaye daraṃ.*'[67]

A change in the situation of a married woman from a lay disciple to a recluse was made possible by acquiring merit in a past birth. The all-inclusive nature of the saṇgha is emphasized by the inclusion of unmarried women in the Order. In the instance of *therī* Selā,[68] she was born to a clansman's household and was married to a man of equal status. She lived a happy married life and became inclined towards religion after the demise of her husband. Once she made a grand offering of a feast to the Buddha and worshipped him. Through this she gained merit and was reborn as a princess. The Master ordained her father, the monarch of the kingdom of Ālavī. The unmarried Selā was at her father's palace and had the opportunity to hear the Master preaching. She was so influenced by the Master that she became a lay disciple. With the passage of time she worked her way towards gaining insight and attained arhantship. Once Māra tried to interrupt her but failed in his attempt.

Another variation of this is seen in the verse of an anonymous sister[69] where we hear the story of the nurse of the Great Pajāpatī. The nurse renounced the world following her mistress but she required twenty-five years to tame the lust of her senses. It was only by practising meditative exercises that she could develop insight.

We also learn about the ordination of 500 sisters under the Elder Paṭācārā.[70] These sisters were born to different clansmen's places and led married lives with children. They all suffered endless grief at the death of their respective children. Overwhelmed with grief they found their way to the Order after hearing the preaching of *therī* Paṭācārā. They renounced their worldly life and practised insight. This clearly emphasizes that the saṇgha was open to members of all clans.

The instance of *thera* Suppiya[71] also makes it apparent that the Order was open to everyone irrespective of class or caste. As a consequence of his past deeds Suppiya was born to a lowly class and was a watchman in a cemetery. Once, he heard the preaching of his friend *thera* Sopāka and was thoroughly influenced. He entered the Order and strove hard to attain arhantship.

In the instance of *thera* Pakkha,[72] the monk suffered from a disease and used to walk like a cripple. Thus, he was named Pakkha (cripple). Due to his immense interest in the Buddhist path, he entered the Order. One day while collecting alms in a neighbouring area, he saw a kite being attacked by other kites for a piece of meat carried in his beak. On seeing this he could see a similarity between this action and human desire and realized its futility. As his insight expanded, he attained arhantship. He said that greed is what leads one to be reborn again and again just like kites come to the ground for meat. To overcome desire is the ultimate happiness—'*Cutā patanti patitā giddhā ca punar āgatā. kataṃ kiccaṃ rataṃ rammaṃ sukhen' anvāgataṃ sukhanti.*'[73]

Thera Kumāra-Kassapa[74] was brought up in the Buddhist vihāra as he was born to his mother after she entered the Order. Later he was reared in the royal household and was known as the Kumāra-Kassapa. As he grew up the king took him to the Buddha so that he could be ordained. Eventually he practised insight and underwent different trials to attain the right path. Later the Master ranked him foremost amongst those who had versatile knowledge.

All the above narratives indicate the inclusive aspect of the saṇgha. Unlike the brahmanical system of *caturāśrama*,[75] the Buddhist saṇgha was far more encompassing. Besides having no fixed age for admission to the saṇgha, caste and class too were of no significance. The sole emphasis was on the attainment of insight by the recluse. This stands sharply in contrast to nuptial ties which were based mainly on the principle of endogamous marriages and certain other factors like, in the case of men for example, physical strength, talent and prowess. The recognition of an institution governed by alternative social principles is significant. While there was no explicit challenge to the institution of marriage except by those adopting the path of renunciation, the implicit challenge of an alternative in the saṇgha is noteworthy.

From the various instances encountered in the choices made by recluses, the influence of the popular appeal of the Buddhist ethos becomes apparent. Unsurprisingly, Bodhisattas feature as outstanding leaders who preached a religion that could accommodate everyone, irrespective of differences. Yet the consent of the elderly figure of the family was a necessity to get admission to the Order. At times the king was seen granting permission to the individual to renounce social life. The king himself could independently choose his partner in marriage and decide to enter the saṇgha. Women, too, often exerted their choice of opting out of the householder's life. This possibly indicated the relative flexibility of the Buddhist saṇgha in comparison to worldly life. However, it would be naïve to presume that androcentrism and misogyny was absent in the saṇgha. In each of the instances where women wished to join the order they had to struggle—on one hand, to break the shackles of the patriarchal world, and on the other, to enter an Order that was highly androcentric.

Hindrances as Reality

The period covered in this volume witnessed the rise of heretical orders questioning Vedic rituals and brahmanical traditions. The institution of the saṇgha stood as an alternative, if not potentially egalitarian, establishment to orthodox brahmanical society. The inclusive spirit of the saṇgha encouraged individuals from all spheres to renounce the social world. However, there were no less obstacles in the path of *nibbāna*. At times the constant connection with the social world in order to obtain alms proved to be an obstacle in the life of the ascetic. The textual description of the presence of women as symbols of lust and seductresses appears everywhere. Women were often considered the reason for ascetics being derailed from the path of religion. Besides, the presence of other heterodox sects (for example, the Ajivikas) often stood as severe hindrances in the path of the *bhikkhu*. Here I will explore the importance of an individual's agency to make choices, and their strength of mind to not be derailed by heterodox preachers. I find it of utmost necessity to locate the past of the misogynist society which stands in contrast to the Buddhist notion that everyone should be free to choose to be happy.

Defining the 'Improper' in Renunciation

There is a common understanding of the 'improper' in the Jātakas, the *Therīgāthā* and the *Theragāthā* regarding liberation. What is worth contemplating is the diversity of the 'improper' that apparently posed a terrible threat to the recluse on the path to salvation. The 'improper' encounters that caused the Brothers to return to worldly life, upon their inability to live the life of a recluse, were widespread. Besides, the inherent qualities of individuals and the disturbing presence of other heretical sects were no less a threat to the smooth running of the saṇgha. This can be compared with the 'improper' relations in marriage that stood in the way of married couples.[76]

The recluse's desire to return to his wife and the past life was common in Buddhist narratives and was constantly warned against by the Master.[77] Many narratives discuss how ascetics suffered because of their desire for their wives or their worldly lives. The Master warned against this by narrating instances from previous births about the danger of cohabiting with women. Here, the evil in women was synonymous with a fatal end. Matrimonial ties in worldly life stood in opposition to the Buddhist path of liberation. Attachment to one's past life often stood as an obstacle to the *thera*'s realization of *nibbāna*. This was perhaps the real reason for Buddhists; sceptical attitude towards *bhikkhus*' wives in their worldly lives.

Projecting women as treacherous and licentious was a common occurrence throughout the Jātaka narratives. Paradoxically, threats from women featured as a hindrance in both the worldly life and the saṇgha that stood as an alternative to it. For instance, many narratives hint at the threat posed by the wives and paramours of hermits even in their secluded existence. In one story the daughter of a treasurer was very unpopular among her maids due to her cruelty.[78] Once, the treasurer's daughter was very rude to her servants and was ruthless in dealing with them. The servants planned to take revenge and left her in distress. In her helpless state, she was rescued by the Bodhisatta. The Bodhisatta was a hermit and lived in the forest. He practised his faith and had renounced worldly life. The woman lured him with all her charms and made the ascetic fall in love with her. Yielding to her pleas, he stayed with her in a border village and earned his living by selling dates. It did not take her long to find a paramour in a robber who attacked their house and imprisoned her. She had the robber brutally torture the Bodhisatta. It was only after some time had passed that the robber realized his folly and killed the lady. The Bodhisatta decided to renounce worldly life once again and returned to the hermitage. Even the robber accompanied him and became a recluse himself. The narrative not only hints at the hindrance of worldly attractions but also describes the inconsistent nature of women, who are never to be trusted.

Archaic notions that perpetuated gender norms were constructed at varied levels in the early Buddhist texts. Women were considered a hindrance to the Brothers even after renouncing worldly life.[79] In one such case a *bhikkhu* was lured by the charm of a well-decked woman. The Buddha, addressing the brethren, said that women stood as a hurdles even to men who had attained the highest honours in the Brotherhood. He mentioned that many wise men were led astray by hearing the mesmerizing voice of women. He described the company of women as a vice for the brethren.

Similar instances hinting at passion and lust coming in the way of practicing religion becomes evident from repeated references to the Buddha's birth stories. A learned brāhmaṇa, well versed in Vedic knowledge, used to teach many young brāhmaṇas. However, he settled down after marriage and became engrossed in all kinds of worldly thoughts.[80] This stood in the way of him gaining wisdom. He started forgetting verses and could not remember the knowledge he had acquired. He went to the Master in Jetavana and came to know that it was lust and passion that had been obstructing his vision.

In order to explain the intensity of demonic power in the charm of women, the Buddha, in one story,[81] recollected events from his past birth. A Brother admitted to the Master that he was charmed by well-dressed women. The Master warned him that women were capable of leading men astray by luring them with their voice, physical gestures and touch.

He remembered that a group of she-goblins had previously tempted a caravan of traders with their charm and brought them under their control.

Repeated examples of *bhikkhus* becoming victims to women while collecting alms were common. In a story, the brethren brought a Brother before the Master. The Brother was mesmerized by a beautiful woman he met during his rounds and had become very disturbed.[82] He became so derailed that he lost all his interest in the Buddhist faith. On realizing the severity of the situation the Master told the brethren that wise men always chose the life of asceticism over worldly pleasures.

We have already seen depictions of the heinous nature of women in several narratives in this chapter. These women seemed to pose a threat to ascetics by their mere presence.[83] We find that even after her death the wife of a landowner in Jetavana remained a constant distraction for him. He was so depressed by her loss that he was unable to lead his regular life. It was only through the Master's intervention that the lay Brother realized the impermanence of worldly relations.

Women attempting to malign the Buddha surface in a narrative from the *Mahā-Paduma-Jātaka*.[84] In Jetavana a few heretics had tried to compete and receive more alms than the Buddhist monastery. They left no stone unturned to tarnish the reputation of the monastery. After repeated failures in maligning the Buddhist order, they made use of a beautiful sister who used to come to the monastery of the heretics. She tried to convince the lay disciples that she spent nights in the Buddhist saṇgha. After quite some time had passed she went to the Buddha where he was preaching. She feigned pregnancy and stated that the child belonged to him. However, what followed this incident was her complete ruination because of her falsehood. In contrast, the Buddhist monastery and the Buddha's fame remained unhindered and, in fact, became more popular with time.

Repeated instances of lust and passion as significant obstacles to the realization of insight indicate the severity of this situation. Another variation of the above narrative features in a story from the *Mudulakkhaṇa-Jātaka*.[85] Here, a *thera*, after renouncing worldly life, joined the Brotherhood. It was only after seeing a woman in revealing attire that he was allured by her. In his troubled state of mind he failed to concentrate on his faith and the Order. He became so disturbed that he lost his peace of mind. It was with the Buddha's assistance that he was able to recover from this state. Restraining passion was not an easy task even for dedicated ascetics. This is evident time and again in the narratives of the Jātakas. The Buddha cites that like an ill-doer, the passionate man is excused neither in hell nor in heaven.[86]

The idea of wisdom in the textual traditions was synonymous with the Buddha. In one story we are told about King Dhanaṇjaya of the Kuru kingdom. He had a brāhmaṇa priest as his temporal and spiritual adviser. Once he enquired about truth and wisdom from him, to which the brāhmaṇa could not provide an answer. He realized that an answer to the king's question could be obtained only from the omnipotent Bodhisatta. He travelled through the entire Jambudīpa but failed to resolve the king's doubts. This is because he kept meeting men who in the throes of passion and thus did not have wisdom or clear vision. This also attests to the role of passion as acute obstacles to wisdom. At last he met a prodigious 7 year old named Sambhava and he, with the Buddha's blessings, found a solution to the king's numerous doubts. The brāhmaṇa rewarded him with riches and the king showered him with great honour.

All these narratives about passion as a terrible threat to the individual's mental serenity indicate the typical perspective and goal of the stories. These instances were selected for the specific purpose of warning recluses and ordinary people about the consequences of 'improper' desire.

Apart from bodily lust the desire for food and comfort often stood as a hurdle in the path to arhantship. A Brother in a story from the *Kuddāla-Jātaka*[87] joined the Brotherhood after tasting sweet food from the bowl of an Elder. He practised the faith for six weeks but desired worldly pleasures after that. He joined and left the saṇgha a number of times, chasing his lust. It was after several such endeavours that he could finally attain arhantship.

The presence of hypocrites in the disguise of a recluse was not rare. We find one such example in a case where an ascetic in Benaras used to dwell in the forest. He was supported by a rich *gahapati*[88] who built the recluse an excellent hermitage in the midst of the forest and considered him a model of goodness. Due to the fear of robbers, the *gahapati* buried a hundred pieces of gold in the hermitage in the custody of the recluse. No sooner did the *gahapati* leave than the recluse thought of taking the gold. He fooled the *gahapati* and left the hermitage after hiding the gold in a river. It was with the intervention of a Bodhisatta that the reality of the wicked ascetic was exposed.

If we turn to evidence from the *Therīgāthā* and *Theragātha* we see how difficult it was for renouncers to tame their passion. The story of the nurse of the Great Pajāpatī, who renounced the world following her mistress, has already been mentioned in this chapter. In another instance, *therī* Sundarī-Nandā[89] was influenced by the Master's preaching and was inspired by the fact that a *bhikkhunī* was assigned a foremost position in meditative power. She went on gaining merit in order to achieve an elevated position in her rebirths. After several rebirths, she was born into a royal family and was well known for her bodily charm. At some point of time she realized that every member of her kin had renounced the world and joined the Buddha's path. Thus, she also considered leaving the world. Yet her choice of renouncing the world was more out of her love for her kin than her devotion to the faith. As a result, she faced several obstacles from within, remaining intoxicated with pride in her physical charm and unable to reflect on insight. However, the Master made her realize the futility of physical beauty and helped her attain insight. Thus, with time, she was able to attain arhantship.

A similar situation arises in the verse of *thera* Uttiya,[90] as we learn about his conversion to the Buddhist path. Once, as he went on his rounds to collect alms, he heard a woman singing. Desire and passion arose in him. Immediately, he diverted himself from desire through the power of meditation.

In the instance of *thera* Kimbila,[91] we discover how the Master taught him a lesson about impermanence by conjuring up an image of a beautiful woman and demonstrated how she passed to old age. By seeing this, the *thera* realized the futility of sensual desires. Eventually he went to the Master, heard his preaching and entered the Order. This parallels the situations where the Master assisted his disciples in dealing with the threat posed by evil partners in marriage.

Often, hindrances on the path of salvation cropped up in varied ways. *Thera* Puṇṇamāsa[92] had renounced the life of a householder after the birth of his son. Soon after his departure his son passed on and his wife became concerned about the inheritance of their property. She did not want it to be passed to the king. Thus, with a great following she went to greet her husband and left no stone unturned to bring him back. However, her attempts failed and she could not influence the *thera* to renounce religious life. He made his opinion about the impermanence of worldly life clear and spoke about the vices of the five hindrances in the way of liberation. These were: the desires of the senses, malevolence, sluggishness, distraction, and perplexity. He described how he could surmount all these obstacles by understanding and following religious norms. By reflecting on them he had realized the temporary existence of the body—'*Pañca nīvaraṇe hitvā yogakkhemassa pattiyādhammādāsaṃ gahetvāna ñāṇadassanam attano paccavekkhiṃ imaṃ kāyaṃ sabbaṃ santarabāhiraṃ, ajjhattañ ca bahiddhā ca tuccho kāyo adissathā 'ti.*'[93]

Another instance of the inner struggle of the *bhikkhu* posing a hindrance to his salvation is evident in the example of *thera* Uttarapāla.[94] Uttarapāla was born to a brāhmaṇa's household. He entered the Order and began pursuing his studies. One day it so happened that he was preoccupied with sensual desires. After a violent mental struggle, he arrested the corrupting mood and attained arhantship. Reflecting on his success he uttered his verse: 'Me seeming wise, forsooth, and spent enough in pondering on the things that make for good. [I] overthrew fivefold desires of sense, bewilders of the world . . . yet did my strength suffice to win'.

Thera Nandaka[95] entered the order after hearing the Master preach. Once by hearing his preaching, 500 *bhikkhunīs* attained arhantship, clearly emphasizing his immense popularity and the influence of the Buddhist discourse at the time. The Master elevated him to the foremost rank amongst the brethren and the sisters. However, one day while going on his rounds to collect alms he came across his wife from his worldly life. She made attempts to lure him but failed. He taught her the norms of the abhorrence and temporality of the body.

All the above examples have tried to present worldly attachments and passion as common hindrances in the path of liberation. Here, the Buddha is considered the Master and his life was more than an exemplary model for the masses. Therefore the portrayal of relations with women as maleficent in the Buddha's life was a severe warning to common folk. In a plethora of instances cited above the Buddhist way of constructing women as seductive and evil forces us to question the all-inclusive nature of the saṇgha. The gendered nature of passion is explicated through the widespread examples of sensual pleasure as an obstacle in the path of the *bhikkhus*, whereas it was only on rare occasion that we learn about a *bhikkhunī*'s sensual passion hindering her way to insight. This can be contrasted with the 'improper' relations in marriages where women faced repeated scorn because of their unfaithful nature. However, adultery in men was considered conventional and was hardly regarded as a vice. In the case of liberation we come across a different situation. Here, conventionally men were victims of worldly desire and rescued by the Master, whereas the examples of passion among *bhikkhunīs* were rare. Thus it can be assumed that women in worldly life were a constant cause of agony for both householder and recluses but they were supposed to tame their minds after joining the Order. Then, quite naturally, the question of a woman being lured by men in worldly life was extremely limited. There is, thus, a difference between the way in which the Jātakas and the *Therīgāthā* represent women; on the other hand, the Jātakas and the *Theragāthā* offer us a broad understanding of women's nature.

Inherent Traits

Personal traits of the renouncers varied and at times were constraints in their path to attain arhantship. This can be compared to the 'proper' traits of individuals necessitated by the Buddhist texts for the successful working of matrimonial alliances. As noted earlier 'improper' characteristics in brides or grooms were responsible for unproductive marriages.[96] Similarly, in representations of renunciation recluses' 'improper' traits stood in the way of them attaining insight. Through the following examples an attempt will be made to indicate the severity of this situation.

Physical stature often played a significant role in the saṇgha as evident from certain narratives in the Jātakas.[97] In one story we come across the venerable Lakuṇtaka, the disciple of the Buddha. He was a famous preacher and everyone wanted to meet him. However, nobody could recognize him as he was of an insignificant stature. He was treated like a dwarf and kept for amusement in the saṇgha. It was with the intervention of the Buddha that the brethren realized their mistake and recognized him as a significant elder. The above example closely parallels the negotiation of matrimonial alliances where physical attributes played a crucial role.[98]

Instances when the human nature of the Brothers was a hindrance in their path were not rare, as exemplified in the following story.[99] The Bodhisatta had a headstrong disciple who had a pet elephant. The Master advised him not to keep the elephant as a pet because once it grew up, they would harm even they ones who fostered and took care of them. The disciple turned a deaf ear to this advice as he was very attached to his pet. Gradually, the elephant grew to be enormous. One day, he turned wild, smashing everything that came in his way. He trampled over the disciple, ending his life. On hearing this, the Master remarked to his followers that it was not harmful to be docile, but that one should never be obstinate.

The nexus between worldly life and the saṅgha—based on the relation of almsgiving by the laity to the Order—led to several conflicts. We learn of an incident where the brethren were in the process of making houses for themselves. Thus, they begged for materials required for the construction.[100] Not only so, they also asked for a servant who would help them in the process of building cells. This annoyed everyone in the vicinity and they began avoiding the brethren. Once, the revered Elder Mahakassapa visited the place and received no alms. He became suspicious and asked the brethren the reason. Later, the Buddha found out about this and rebuked them for such conduct. Here, it is clear that the traits of the *bhikkhus* stood in their way of accumulating alms. This provide contrast to the world of domesticity where individual behaviour also often leads to conflict.

At times the selfishness of the inmates of the saṅgha stood as a hindrance on their religious path. Brothers with immoral characters were common. One such *thera* named Upananda was ordained to the faith but was very greedy. Two Brothers in a monastery could not divide a fine blanket between them. They asked Upananda to evenly share it between them. However, Upananda took the blanket away, claiming it as his rightful share instead of sharing it between the Brothers. He said he deserved the blanket as he held great wisdom. However, this was brought to the notice of the Master and he explained how it was wrong for a Brother to be greedy and covetous. This provides a parallel to instances of selfish partners in marriage, who were also shown the right path by the Master.[101]

Another instance of greed features in the story of a *bhikkhu* who he lived in a forest on the border of a village and received a large amount of alms every day.[102] This too provides a parallel to the greedy partner represented as 'improper' in nuptial ties.[103] After a month the village was burned down and the people hardly had anything to sustain themselves. Therefore, they could hardly offer any alms to the Brother. Eventually he lost interest in the path of religion owing to the scarcity of alms. However, the Master made him realize that an ascetic ought to set aside his covetous ways and remain content with the bare minimum. Greed among the Brothers was often shunned as destructive to the path of faith. The texts discuss how bodily passion was the main cause of ascetics getting derailed from the path of religion. Similarly, greed for material gains was also warned against by the Master.

The Master often could be seen admonishing greedy inmates in the saṇgha, as is evident in a narrative where a Brother seems dissatisfied with his state of asceticism. He was only interested in food and other luxuries.[104] He took immense delight if meat was ever served to him. Through the Master's intervention the *thera* recollected his past birth and his lowness was explicated.

Selfishness and conflict for alms were no rare events.[105] One story tells us of a sister in the Order who used to warn all her companions not to go to a certain area to collect alms. She did this so that she would be the only one to receive all the alms from that area. One day she met with an accident and all the other sisters came to know that she used to collect alms from the area that she warned them not to visit. This is indicative of an ironic representation of the 'improper' in renunciation.

On the contrary we also hear the example of a Tathāgata[106] who stayed with a brāhmaṇa for three months in order to obtain alms from him.[107] However, owing to the influence of the evil spirit Māra, he failed to receive alms even for a single day from the brāhmaṇa. Hence, through the strength of his mind, he gave up his covetous ways and lived on the bare minimum required for sustenance. Here we are presented with a clear juxtaposition of 'proper' and 'improper' behaviour among the bretheren.

The impurity of the soul has been repeatedly emphasized in Buddhist texts as 'improper'. This impurity inevitably leads to fatal consequences. In one instance, *thera* Uttiya[108] became a wanderer in search of bliss. He arrived at the place where the Master preached and, after listening to his teachings, he entered the Order. Yet, due to the impurity of his soul he could not attain his goals. Later, the Master taught him the right way to find bliss. Uttiya eventually overcame all obstacles and attained arhantship.

At another level, the Master pointing at sins of all kinds as hindrances for mankind is exemplified in the story about the 500 citizens of Sāvatthī who heard the Buddhist law and renounced the world.[109] However they fell prey to the thoughts of sin deemed to be 'improper' on the path to attain arhantship. The Buddha explained to them that there was nothing such as petty sins and that all sins were to be subdued as they were equally harmful for mankind. Here the emphasis on rectifying 'improper' traits in an individual prior to attaining spiritual wisdom in religion is identical to situations where the father attempted to check his daughter's virginity before her entry into married life.[110] This is a contrast to renunciation where thoughts of sin are equally 'improper' irrespective of gender, whereas, in most of the instances of matrimonial alliance it is only the bride's purity that is highlighted.

'Improper' conduct by women has been clearly represented as a terrible threat to the Buddhist saṇgha. In one story we learn of the daughter of a citizen of Sāvatthī.

She was supposed to be a lucky charm for her future husband but no one chose to marry her. As a result, her mother decided to entrap a Sākiyan ascetic and bring him back to worldly life. She found her prey in a young man who had joined the Brotherhood. However, with time he had lost interest in religion and deviated from the path. One day he came across the old woman, who offered him alms. She asked him to visit her regularly. Thus, her daughter got the chance to enamour him with all her charms. The man was overpowered with passion and thought of renouncing the life of an ascetic. However, with the intervention of the Master he was made to realize his imbecilic actions and ultimately refrained from falling prey to the woman.

In another story we learn of a girl from a reputed family who had embraced asceticism. The moment she saw the enlightened image of the Master, she remembered her previous birth.[111] In her former existence she was one of the Bodhisatta's wives. She also remembered that though many among the wives were well-mannered, there were others who were ill-natured. She perceived that she had held a few grudges against her husband in her previous birth. Recollecting this she became uncontrollably depressed and wept aloud. On seeing her condition the brethren questioned the Master about the reason for her ceaseless grief. To this the Master explained that she was ashamed of recounting her previous birth where she had sinned against her husband.

The above narrative stands sharply in contrast to tales of male ascetics pining for their worldly life. We often find those narratives in a different setting, with the Brothers lost in passion and disoriented on remembering the wife of their past life. However, the situation with the female novice is portrayed with visible differences. Here, she is seen lamenting the sin she committed against her husband. Besides, the Buddha, instead of admonishing her for brooding over her past worldly life, was more lenient towards her.

Hindrances in the path of renunciation were numerous for *bhikkhunīs*. In the instance of *therī* Subhā this obstacle was her charming physical features.[112] Subhā had a strong inclination towards the Buddhist faith. Very soon she realized the bane of the physical senses and found renunciation to be her only path forward. She entered the Order under the Great Pajāpatī. Once, she came across a youth in a mango grove who was enamoured by her. She declared to him the bane of sensual pleasures and her ideas about renunciation. Yet he could not be cured and was lured by her lovely eyes. To teach him about the impermanence of physical charms she extracted her eyes and handed them to him. Shocked, he asked her for forgiveness. Later she was elevated to the highest status by the Master. This clearly hints at her 'proper' behaviour as represented by the text.

In another instance, it becomes clear how the malignant power of Māra could be impeded by a dedicated and strong-willed man. This is evident in the instance of *thera* Nandiya.[113] Nandiya left the world under the Master along with *thera* Aniruddha and because of his wisdom in his past life he attained arhantship soon after. However, Māra, the evil spirit tried to frighten him with his terrible form. This was all in vain, as the *thera* drove him away with his insight and told him about the impossibility of derailing him. In contrast to the above instance of a determined *therī* who had to cause physical harm to herself to convince the man of her disinterest in sensual pleasure, the *thera* was able to overcome Māra with relative ease.

At times physical illness stood in the way of *bhikkhus* pursuing religion. This becomes evident in the case of *thera*

Sīvaka.[114] He was instructed by his mother to follow his maternal uncle, who had left the world to join the Order. Due to his aspiration to join the Buddhist faith and the bidding of his mother, he left the world. Once he fell ill at the outskirts of the village. As he found no medicines, he could not return to the Order. The Elder went to find him, cured him and took him back to the forest. He attained arhantship soon after and realized that worldly bondage was 'improper'.

The treatment envisaged for supporting parents hardly varied in either marriage or renunciation. In a verse from the *Theragatha*, we see that a Brother retained close connection to the lay world and supported his mother.[115] Although his relation with worldly life was considered a hindrance on the path of asceticism, the Master appreciated that the Brother was supporting his aged mother and considered it an appropriate gesture. Similarly, in previously related narrative[116] we have seen how a caring son asked his wife to leave the house as she complained about his aged mother. He made it clear that his mother was old and could not survive without his support. In both instances the tone of the Buddhist texts indicates the supporting parents was considered a 'proper' gesture.

Bodily charm was treated differently in marriage and renunciation. Physical charm was apparently a prerequisite in a woman for matrimonial alliances, whereas, in the life of *bhikkhunīs*, infatuation with the same was considered a vice. In the instance of *therī* Khemā,[117] we learn about her repeated rebirths due to her meritorious deeds that included almsgiving to the Buddhist faith. Not only did she donate food and her own hair, there are records of her making a great park for the Buddhist saṇgha in her respective births. Once she was born into a royal household and became the consort of King Bimbisāra. However, she remained infatuated with her physical charms and had no inclination towards religion. The Master made her realize the impermanence of her bodily grace. Perceiving her imbecilic attitude she tried to reflect on herself to gain insight. Yet, she still faced obstacles as Māra, the evil spirit took on a youthful form and tried to lure her with sensuous ideas.

Another variation indicating that physical charm was fatal to the path of renunciation features in the case of *therī* Puṇṇā.[118] Due to Puṇṇā's inclination towards the Buddhist faith, she listened to the teachings of a *bhikkhunī* and entered the Order. Very soon she became well versed in the Tripiṭakas and was considered an expert. However, pride was an obstacle on her way to liberation. Due to her karma she was reborn in the household of Anātha-pindika as a slave. Through her extreme sincerity and loyalty to the faith she won the Master's confidence and was admitted to the Order.

Unlike matrimonial alliances where physical charm and appearance played a potent role, here we come across the notion of inner traits as essential for renunciation. *Thera* Vasabha,[119] born to a Licchavī king, was won over by the majesty of the Buddha and left the world. Eventually he attained arhantship and received gifts from his patrons. He was misunderstood as self-indulgent by many ordinary people. There also dwelt in the vicinity another deceptive *bhikkhu* who fooled people by pretending to be simple and content with very little. Then Sakka asked *thera* Vasabha what a fraud does. Vasabha said that none can be judged by outer appearance. It is only inner qualities that created one's true identity on the path of salvation.

The discussion in this section indicates the heterogeneous possibilities of hindrances stemming from worldly life. Indeed, the Buddhist tradition clearly indicated the vices of conjugal life as potent obstacles on the path of religion. Pining for the same was deemed 'improper' for recluses. However, there were obstacles beyond sensual pleasure that were no less a barrier. For instance, an individual's personal traits were as much an obstacle on the way to arhantship. The parallels between the recluse and the householder allow us to perceive these 'improper' personal traits as problematic in both the contexts. Hence, in this case a common strand of Buddhist ethics seems to run through the Jātakas, the *Therīgāthā* and the *Theragāthā*.

Heretical Sects

The idea of adulterous relations time and again proved to be a serious threat to marriages in the Buddhist textual traditions.[120] The presence of the 'other' has been vehemently opposed in the Buddhist texts as a hindrance to the thriving of nuptial ties. In most of these instances women were admonished severely for being unfaithful. However, turning to renunciation we find the presence of the brahmanical religion and other heretical sects as the inimical 'other' to Buddhist religion. At times the thriving popularity of Buddhism was challenged and thwarted by other sects and practices. This becomes clear in the following narratives. Instances of the Brothers facing disdain from lay followers were not rare. One such example features[121] a Brother who was revered in the neighbouring village for his skill in meditation. People, pleased with his manner, constructed a dwelling for him in the woods and bestowed him with great honour. However, with the passage of time the villagers forsook him for other heretical sects. Later he returned to the monastery and conveyed his experience to the Master. He told him how it had become difficult to stay with people who could not differentiate good from evil. This is a close parallel to the betrayed husbands who expressed their grief to the Master about their unfaithful wives and regretted not listening to his advice.[122]

Brothers returning to their worldly lives, after being unable to live the life of a recluse, were also not rare. However, in one story (also discussed previously in this volume) an adherent of the Buddha not only left the saṇgha for worldly life but also spread falsehoods against the Buddha and his doctrine.[123] Later, the Buddha came to know about this from Sāriputta and explained the Brother's folly to him. This was no less a threat for the reputation of the saṇgha.

We also come across instances where *annatithiyas* (followers of other sects) created trouble and maligned the Buddha's doctrine. In the story of Devadatta, he, along with his 500 followers left no stone unturned to slander the image of the Buddha and break up the saṇgha.[124] He made repeated attempts to do this but failed every time.

Another variation of the above instance can be traced to the story of Devadatta,[125] who plotted to kill the Buddha out of sheer jealousy.[126] The other heterodox religious sects were a constant threat to the Buddhist saṇgha. This is clear from the hostile attitude of the sectarian faiths towards the huge share of alms received by the saṇgha. We learn about the generous alms received by the Buddhist saṇgha in the region of Jetavana.[127] This enraged the sectarian faiths. They held a meeting to find a solution to their diminished honour. They decided to establish a monastery in the vicinity of the Buddhist saṇgha in order to compete with it. In the process of making this rival settlement, they bribed the king of Kosala for his support. The Buddha tried to bring this issue to the king's notice. However, each time his disciples tried, they were turned down by the king. It was the Buddha who eventually met the king and made him realize his misdeeds.

Once in the town of Rājagaha, Sāriputta lived with his disciples and Devadatta lived in a nearby region with a group of wicked followers.[128] Disputes between these two groups surfaced regarding a perfumed golden robe donated by a trader. Devadatta won the support of the majority and claimed ownership over the robe. However, the Buddha recalled a similar incident from his past birth. He explained that this was not the first time that Devadatta had taken the garb of a saint to hid his evil qualities. On many such occasions, he had managed to fool people with his falsehoods. Thus the Buddhist narratives distinguish between the 'proper' and 'improper' and the potent threat by the inimical 'other'.

The hostile presence of Devadatta is omnipresent in the narratives of the Jātakas. We often come across his different inimical activities against the Buddha and his saṇgha. One such instance is described where the brethren reminded Devadatta of all the Master's amicable gestures towards him.[129] They made him aware of the assistance he received from the Buddha at times of need. However, Devadatta turned a deaf ear to all of them and denied their claims.

In other narrative, when King Ajātasattu killed his father, Bimbisara, Devadatta went to him and asked for a favour. He said that in the same way that the king that committed patricide to have his desired fulfilled, he too wanted to have the learned Master, Dasabala, killed and become the Buddha himself. The king assisted him in order to conceal his own sins.[130] Accumulating a number of archers for the purpose of killing the Buddha, Devadatta asked them to carry out his orders. The archers tried to follow the order diligently but each of them failed in their attempt. They were so overpowered by the Buddha's aura that they gave themselves over to faith instead of killing him. The hostile presence of the other heterodox sects in opposition to the Buddhist saṇgha is manifested with the constant endeavour of Devadatta to kill the Buddha. However, each time he failed to accomplish his mission.

The narratives even speak about the demise of Devadatta, which was celebrated with great pomp. It took nine months for Devadatta to plan the murder of the Buddha.[131] Ironically it was Devadatta who met a tragic end in the process. Many people rejoiced at his end. The shrewd tone of the Buddhist text becomes clear through the celebration of the tragic end of an individual who was considered a potential threat to the Buddha. This parallels the celebration of the demolishment of demonic power represented by powerful women in worldly life.[132]

Besides life threats to the Buddha the heretics at times created hindrances in the process of alms distribution.[133] A family at Sāvatthī used to distribute alms among the disciples of the Buddha as well as the heretics. Often there used to be conflicts regarding the distribution of alms. However, a plan for proper distribution of wealth was followed and the heretics could not prevent the alms from reaching the Buddha's saṇgha.

However, such instances of threats by sectarian faiths and the recognition of a rival 'other' could hardly be featured in the *Therīgāthā* and the *Theragāthā*, although we can note the presence of other sects and conversion to Buddhism from the same as a common practice. The paucity of references to threats indicates the different audiences addressed by the respective texts. The Jātakas probably targeted a wider section of the population to whom the portrayal of other sects as a potential threat was the need of the time. But the *Therīgāthā* and the *Theragāthā* had restricted audiences, specifically *bhikkhus*, *bhikkhunīs* and lay followers. It can be assumed that this group of people was already aware of the other sects and accordingly embraced the Buddhist faith. Therefore, it was not essential to focus on the heinous activities of other sects in these texts.

Resolution of Conflicts

Apart from the threat posed by other heretical sects, the conversion of the same to the Buddhist faith was widespread. This opens before us the diverse possibilities of conflict resolution in the Buddhist texts. This can be compared with instances of strife in marriages and the representation of resolutions sought in the texts. Although the notion of marriage and renunciation in the Buddhist texts are polarized, the resolutions of conflicts were, at times, identical.

The internal strife amongst heretical sects brings forth a lot of issues of the particular period. This will be discussed through the following examples. For instance, being derailed from the path of the faith under the wrong influence was rampant.[134] Devadatta, a rival to the Master manipulated King Ajātasattu to gain his patronage. Thus, he and his followers used to amass luxuries and worldly comforts without having to collect alms. Once, Devadatta's disciples invited a follower from the Buddhist monastery to the palace, luring him with an abundance of food. When the Master became aware of this he guided the disciple back to the righteous path. These instances hint at the wrong influences that precluded the recluse from choosing the right path. Clearly, this story can be seen simultaneously reinforcing and questioning the integrity of the *bhikkhus* in the saṇgha. This is similar to the conflict resolution conducted by the Buddha for failed marriages, where the partner showing signs of incorrect behaviour is shown the right way by the Buddha.[135]

The Buddhist texts work with the aim of protesting against Vedic rituals. Therefore the example of the fire sacrifice by brahmanical norms was widespread in the Order. The brethren talked about the false asceticism practised by brahmanical recluses.[136] The Master said that even in earlier times wise men tried to practise the fire sacrifice but soon became aware of its futility. Here we can trace the start opposition of Buddhism to other faiths. Not only so, the negation of the other faith by the Buddha was done in a subtle way, i.e. by implying that members of the brahmanical faith themseves realized the futility of the fire sacrifice. This can be compared to marriages where the wife is categorized as evil and beyond recovery. The husband is made aware of this by the Buddha and shown the vices of worldly attraction.[137]

The instance of *therī* Naduttarā[138] is interesting in this context. She was born to a brāhmaṇa's family and, upon learning the teachings of the Niganthas (unbound or free brethren, usually understood to mean the Jains), entered their Order. As a renowned speaker, she debated with Elder Mahā-Moggallāna of the Buddhist faith. However, she was defeated by him and thereupon listened to his advice. Later, she entered the Buddhist Order and in the long run attained arhantship. This is similar to the instance of the learned daughters who were asked to only get married to the layperson who could defeat them and, if a learned man defeated them, to become his disciple.[139] The reinforcment of the superiority of the Buddhist religion over the Niganthas is clearly visible in this narrative. The differences between both sects have been conveniently resolved by representing the upper hand of the Buddhist faith and the conversion of the *therī* to the same. However, the conversion of the *therī* from the brāhmaṇical religion to the Niganthas and then to the Buddhist faith is also indicative of a flexible and complex religious process.

Another instance of conflict resolution through conversion features in the instance of *therī* Kuṇḍalakesā[140] who converted from the Jain faith to the Buddhist order. Kuṇḍalakesā was born to a royal treasurer. Once she fell in love on seeing a king's prisoner. She was so love-struck that her doting father bribed the king's guard and released the prisoner for his daughter. However, the thief, on meeting the lady was lured by her precious ornaments and made plans to rob her. All his plans failed as Kuṇḍalakesā outsmarted him and saved herself. She decided to join the Jain order and gained wisdom. At a later point of time she was defeated in a debate by a Buddhist elder. Hearing the teachings of the Master she converted from the Jain order and entered the Buddhist faith. A contrasting situation features in the instance of courtesan Sāma,[141] who left her trade and eloped with a robber. On being betrayed by the thief, she returned to her trade.

Another instance of conversion to the Buddhist faith is seen in the case of *thera* Ajjuna,[142] who was influenced by the Jains and entered their order at a very young age. He desired to attain salvation. However, he could hardly find anything to satisfy his quest. His inner conflict was resolved on meeting the Master and entering the Buddhist order. Then he uttered his verse after attaining arhantship: 'O wonder that I found the power to draw, Myself forth from the waters on dry land. Borne drifting on the awful flood I learnt, to know the Truths, their truth to understand.'

In another instance *therī* Mittakālī[143] was born to a brāhmaṇa's family and as she reached a mature age she developed an inclination towards the Buddhist faith and entered the Order. For a long time she was fond of gifts and the luxuries of the material world. Gradually, she became quarrelsome. However, in a later birth she reflected on all her past flaws and gained insight. She attained arhantship soon after this. Here too the resolution in the nature of the *therī* was sought through reflection on insight and her discovering past flaws.

Thera Koṭṭhita[144] was born to a brāhmaṇa's household and attained all the accomplishments of a brāhmaṇa by learning the three Vedas. However, on hearing the Master's preaching, he was so influenced that he entered the Order. He used to question the great *theras* and, eventually, became proficient in insight. In his verse he declared the bliss of emancipation and of the power to do away with sensual trysts. This parallels the situation where the Buddha advised his disciples to stay away from worldly attractions.[145]

Another instance of conversion to the Buddhist faith from the brāhmaṇa household surfaces in the example of *thera* Adhimutta,[146] who was discontented with brahmaṇical wisdom. He once witnessed the majesty of the Buddha at a presentation at Jeta Grove. Thus, he became inclined towards the Buddha's teachings and joined the Order. He also began to admonish the corrupted *bhikkhus* in the Order. Interestingly, this narrative juxtaposes the superior teaching of the Buddha calling for conversion from the brahmanical order with the presence of corrupt *bhikkhus* in the saṇgha. Here, conflict resolution was sought in the new entrant to the saṇgha who, in spite of lacking seniority, admonished the corrupt *bhikkhus* already present in the Order. This reminds us of the failed marriages where the cheated partner admonished his unfaithful wife and married again.[147] What becomes evident in both cases is the fact that the new convert to the saṇgha and the cheated husband decided to punish the evildoer instead of quitting the institution of the saṇgha and marriage, respectively.

Lack of respect among the brethren in the saṇgha has been severely discouraged by the Master. In a story from the *Tittira-Jātaka,*[148] a monastery was built for the brethren under the patronage of Anātha-piṇḍika. The disciples occupied each of the rooms as per their convenience and no room was left for the Elder Sāriputta. One day, the Buddha was taken aback by the strange behaviour of the Brothers. He immediately enquired about the distribution of lodgings and other basic amenities. He then discovered their hierarchical idea of dividing the superior quality of alms received. The Buddha corrected them and emphasized the concept of seniority as the only criterion for distributing alms in the monastery. He told them about the value of mutual respect for the maintenance of the Brotherhood.

In a verse from the *Theragatha, thera* Subhūta[149] renounced the householder's life and joined the sectarian faith. Soon he realized that nothing in the Order was genuine. Eventually, he was influenced by the bliss enjoyed by the *theras* of the Buddhist sect and thought of entering the Buddhist order. With time he developed insight and attained arhantship. In his verse he expressed the sufferings of self-mortification by following the wrong path. The flexibility of conversion to the Buddhist faith in repeated instances arising out of a recluse's inner conflict suggests that these texts aimed to establish the Buddhist religion as the superior faith in the ultimate quest for truth.

The menace of wrong guidance was not rare in the saṇgha. Instances of Brothers facing delays and hurdles in attaining arhantship because of a perpetual wait to meet the Master were quite common. In the narrative of a goldsmith,[150] he was misguided by Sāriputta and could not attain arhantship despite his sincere endeavours. On seeing this, Sāriputta took him to the Buddha to find the reason for the delay. The Buddha pointed out the wrong practice in meditating and soon the goldsmith attained arhantship under the Buddha's guidance. All these possibilities are indicative of the fact that perils in the saṇgha were not rare; however, the same could be surmounted with the intervention of the Master. This is in contrast to failed relationships in worldly life where conflict due to adulterous women was beyond recovery as they could be avoided but not mended.[151]

Parallely, in the *Theragāthā*, in the instance of *thera* Gavaccha,[152] we hear of the strife among *bhikkhus* in the saṇgha. Gavaccha did not side with the contentious groups and developing insight, ultimately attaining arhantship. He was highly disappointed by the *bhikkhus*' quarrelsome nature and realized it would be heinous to involve himself in such strife. He focused on his own path as he believed that the Buddha's path could only be realized through peace, which he proclaimed in his verse.

There were various other kinds of predicaments faced by the Brothers in the stories of the Buddha's different births. For instance, in one narrative we learn that some members of the senior brethren misguided the novices on the path of religion. One *thera* was influenced by listening to the Master preach and joined the Order. [153] After a few days of staying with the senior brethren, he realized the impossibility of learning every lesson on morality. Accordingly, he thought of going back to the worldly life he once renounced. However, after being asked by the Master about his inconvenience, he mentioned his limitations. The Master immediately realized that he had been misguided by the brethren in the saṇgha. He taught the novice the simplicity of the faith and enabled him to attain arhantship.

At times, conflict in the saṇgha had far-reaching consequences and the accused could become the object of justified confrontation by the fuming brethren. The establishment of the saṇgha had differences and parallels with worldly establishments. We find parallels to worldly tiffs in the Buddhist order as well. In many of the narratives we came across rival sects to Buddhism; however, internal strife in the order was no less. A certain Brother in the saṇgha tried to puzzle Sāriputta by questioning him unnecessarily.[154] He believed that by embarrassing Sāriputta he would gain an elevated status among the brethren. However, he failed to realize his and was turned out from the saṇgha by the Brothers. Here, conflict resolution took on a different mode. Instead of the Buddha rectifying this blunder, the Brothers in the saṇgha took the ultimate decision to throw the *bhikkhu* out of the Order. This parallels the instance of a married woman who was ultimately rejected by both her husband and her lover for her dishonest nature and was put to shame in the end.[155]

An instance of a wicked disciple features in the story of the Elder Mahākassapa. The Elder had two disciples;[156] one of them used to serve him but the other was cunning and used to take the credit for this. When the reality of the situation was revealed to Mahākassapa, he immediately made the disciple aware of his misconduct. However, the disciple took this as an offence. He harboured a grudge against Mahākassapa and burnt down his hut. Later, the Buddha came to know about this incident and advised Mahākassapa to stay alone rather than being surrounding himself with evil company. Here, the resolution sought by the Master was similar to that in disputed marriages where he advised parting with bad company as the only means to ward off conflict.[157]

In the case of *thera* Belaṭṭhakāni[158] we learn about his admission to the Order. However, while he practised insight in the forest, he became sluggish and rough in his speech.

Thereby, he could not achieve the right state of mind. It was only after the Master admonished him that he was able to return to the perfect track and, soon after, attained arhantship. Another narrative depicting the gradual transition of a sincere Brother into someone who stopped striving on the path of religion features in the story from the *Saṁvara-Jātaka*.[159] A young man of Sāvatthī renounced the world on hearing the preaching of the Master. Sāvatthī was full of strength, adaptive and hard-working. He was quick to learn the divisions of the *Pātimokkha* (rules of the *Vinaya Pitaka*). He started dwelling in the forest and practised varied forms of penances. However, at a certain point of time he decided to relax and stopped striving to attain liberation. The entire brethren was dissatisfied with him and took him to the Master. He was then made to realize the significance of strenuous effort by the Master. Like an indolent householder, an inactive *bhikkhu* too was a source of contempt among the brethren. Interestingly, it was the Master who played the role of a reformer for both the householder and the *bhikkhu*.

Conclusion

Whether liberation as an idea justifies the concept of 'beyond' in the married life of the householder is not immediately apparent. Yet, in this chapter we have dealt with two crucial assumptions in this context using examples of similarities and contrasts. Various examples of individual exercising choices to opt out of social life are notable. These remind us about the notions of consent and conflict faced by the individual before entering matrimonial alliances.

Although there were variations in the implementation of choice for recluses, the Buddha was regarded as the most influential figure in the Order. In the case of *bhikkhus* who attempted to renounce the saṇgha and return to the social world, the Buddha's intervention in preventing them from doing the same is quite visible. This raises questions regarding the democratic aspect of the notion of liberation. However, it is worth mentioning that *bhikkhunīs* were hardly seen attempting to return to domestic life, unlike the *bhikkhus*. We have learnt through the verses of the *therīs* that renouncing domestic life was more difficult for them than for the *theras* for whom this process was more conventional. Ironically, in many instances it was common to learn about the *bhikkhus*' desire for the worldly life of passion and to hear of their lack of integrity. By contrast, we hardly hear of the *bhikkhunīs*' desire to return to their past lives. This may have been because the saṇgha was relatively less systematically organized on the principle of gender compared to worldly life. Or perhaps because the saṇgha was a last resort for *therīs* and not a traditional option. It can be presumed that *therīs* had to struggle to find a space in the androcentric Order. Therefore, returning to one's past life was never considered a viable option.

At times, passion obstructed *theris*' way to *nibbāna* but they could overcome the same through their strong will. On the contrary, the *bhikkhus*' desire to return to their past lives and their desire for sensual pleasure was widespread and it was only through the Master's intervention that they could be stopped from leaving the Order. Based on this, one can assume that both the patriarchal society and the androcentric Order were flexible enough for men and made space for their occasional vulnerabilities.

While comparing the Jātakas, the *Therīgāthā* and the *Theragāthā*, it becomes apparent that the choice of renouncing worldly ties was not represented uniformly. In contrast to the Jātakas, the *Therīgāthā* lays more stress on the issue of rebirth. Often, an individual could gain merit by exhibiting gratitude to the Buddhist order and being reborn in more fortunate circumstances. Even sins were neutralized by good karma in the *Therīgāthā*, whereas in the *Theragāthā* we are presented with the recluse's natural tendency to embrace the Buddhist faith. Despite the fact that the Jātakas, *Therīgāthā* and the *Theragāthā* are a part of the Buddhist textual genre and assumed to be penned by monks with a strong focus on the Buddhist ethos, there are clear intertextual variations. For instance, in the *Therīgāthā* and the *Theragāthā* we exclusively come across success stories of monks and nuns attaining arhantship. This can be compared to the narratives of the Jātakas, where diverse possibilities are taken into account and we learn about innumerable failures on the path of renunciation alongside stories of success.

NOTES

1. Richard Gombrich, *Theravada Buddhism: A Social History of Ancient Benares to Modern Colombo*, Abingdon: Routledge, 2006, p. 1.
2. Uma Chakravarti, *Everyday Lives, Everyday Histories: Beyond the Kings and Brahmanas of 'Ancient' India*, New Delhi: Tulika Books, 2006, p. 195.
3. Ibid., p. 193.
4. Kumkum Roy, 'Worlds Within and Worlds Without: Representations of the Sangha in "Popular" Tradition', in *Looking Within, Looking Without: Exploring Households in the Subcontinent through Time*, ed. Kumkum Roy, New Delhi: Primus Books, 2015, p. 287.
5. See Chapter 1.
6. Ibid.
7. See story no. 301.
8. E.B. Cowell, ed., *The Jātakas*, New Delhi: Munshiram Manoharlal, 2002, *Makhādeva-Jātaka*, story no. 9.
9. Cowell, *Sukhavihāri-Jātaka*, story no. 10.
10. Cowell, *Yuvañjaya-Jātaka*, story no. 460.
11. Cowell, *Mūga-Pakkha-Jātaka*, story no. 538.

12. Cowell, *Nigrodhamiga-Jātaka*, story no. 12.
13. See story no. 454.
14. Rhys Davids, *Psalms of the Early Buddhists*, London: Pali Text Society and New York: Luzac and Co., 1964, canto 1, part I, commentary I, verse 1.
15. A reference could be made to the Jātakas, where the Buddha is seen to be reborn several times.
16. A comparison is made in the commentary with the way Visākhā introduced Dhammadinnā to the Order.
17. Davids, *Psalms of the Early Buddhists*, canto 2, commentary XX, verse 21–2.
18. Ibid., canto 1, part 8, commentary LXV, verse 76.
19. Ibid., canto 1, part 8, commentary LXXIX, verse 79.
20. Ibid., canto 2, part 3, commentary CXLV, verse 169–70.
21. Oldenberg and Pischel, *Thera- and Theri-gatha*, verse 169–70, http://gretil.sub.uni-goettingen.de/gretil/2_pali/1_tipit/2_sut/5_khudd/theragou.htm.
22. Cowell, *Devadhamma-Jātaka*, story no. 6.
23. See V. Fausboll, ed., *The Jātakas Together with its Commentaries*, vol. 1, London: Trubner & Co., 1877–96, story no. 6.
24. See Chapter 3.
25. Cowell, *Asitābhū-Jātaka*, story no. 234. Already discussed in detail in Chapter 2.
26. Davids, *Psalms of the Early Buddhists*, canto 5, commentary XL, verse 77–8.
27. Oldenberg and Pischel, *Thera- and Theri-gatha*, verse 77–81, http://gretil.sub.uni-goettingen.de/gretil/2_pali/1_tipit/2_sut/5_khudd/therigou.htm.
28. See Cowell, *Jātakas*, story no. 4.
29. Davids, *Psalms of the Early Buddhists*, canto 13, commentary LXIX, verse 312–37.
30. See Cowell, *Jātakas*, story no. 301.
31. Cowell, *Sāma-Jātaka*, story no. 540.
32. Cowell, *Sīlavīmaṁsana-Jātaka*, story no. 86.
33. See Cowell, *Jātakas*, story no. 66.
34. Davids, *Psalms of the Early Buddhists*, canto 7, commentary CCXXVI, verse 473–9.
35. See story no. 201 and Davids, *Psalms of the Early Buddhists*, cantos 7, verse 459–65.

36. Davids, *Psalms of the Early Buddhists*, canto 16, commentary CLXLVIII, verse 705–25.
37. Ibid., canto 1, part 1, commentary V, verse 5.
38. See story no. 200.
39. Cowell, *Losaka-Jātaka*, story no. 41.
40. See story no. 211.
41. Cowell, *Maṭṭa-Kuṇḍali-Jātaka*, story no. 449.
42. Davids, *Psalms of the Early Buddhists*, canto 2, commentary XXVIII, verse 37–8
43. See story no. 354.
44. Davids, *Psalms of the Early Buddhists*, canto 1, part 2, commentary XX, verse 20.
45. Ibid., canto 1, part 11, commentary CIII.
46. Ibid., canto 1, part 2, commentary XV, verse 15.
47. Ibid., canto 3, commentary CLXXIV, verse 231–3.
48. Cowell, *Gumbiya-Jātaka*, story no. 366.
49. See story no. 306.
50. Cowell, *Gijja-Jātaka*, story no. 427.
51. See story no. 211.
52. Cowell, *Lomahaṁsa-Jātaka*, story no. 94.
53. Cowell, *Tipallattha-Miga-Jātaka*, story no. 16.
54. There are different categories of offences, as mentioned in the *Vinaya Piṭaka*. A *Pācittiya* offence required confession and absolution.
55. Cowell, *Māluta-Jātaka*, story no. 17.
56. Davids, *Psalms of the Early Buddhists*, canto 2, part 12, commentary CXXVII, verse 133–4.
57. Ibid., canto 2, part 12, commentary CXXIX, verse 137–8.
58. Oldenberg and Pischel, *Thera- and Theri-gatha*, verse 137–8, http://gretil.sub.uni-goettingen.de/gretil/2_pali/1_tipit/2_sut/5_khudd/theragou.htm.
59. Cowell, *Kuṇḍaka-kucchi-sindhava-Jātaka*, story no. 254.
60. See story no. 318.
61. Cowell, *Mahā-sutasoma-Jātaka*, story no. 537.
62. See story no. 419.
63. Davids, *Psalms of the Early Buddhists*, canto 2, commentary XXII, verse 25–6.
64. Ibid., canto 2, commentary XXIII, verse 27–8.
65. See story no. 306.

66. Davids, *Psalms of the Early Buddhists*, canto 2, commentary XXV, verse 31–2.
67. See Charles Hallisey, tr., *Therīgāthā: Poems of the First Buddhist Women*, London: Murty Classical Library of India, 2015, verse 32.
68. Davids, *Psalms of the Early Buddhists*, canto 3, commentary XXXV, verse 57–9.
69. Ibid., canto 5, commentary XXXVIII, verse 67–71.
70. Ibid., canto 6, commentary L, verse 127–32.
71. Ibid., canto 1, part 4, commentary XXXII, verse 32.
72. Ibid., canto 1, part 7, commentary LXIII, verse 63.
73. Oldenberg and Pischel, *Thera- and Theri-gatha*, verse 63, http://gretil.sub.uni-goettingen.de/gretil/2_pali/1_tipit/2_sut/5_khudd/theragou.htm.
74. Davids, *Psalms of the Early Buddhists*, canto 2, part 4, commentary CXLVI, verse 201–2.
75. *Caturāśrama* refers to the four stages of life in Hinduism. The *brahmachari*, marked by devotion; *grihasta*, or married life; *vanprastha*, or withdrawal from material life; and *sanyasi*, renouncement.
76. As discussed in Chapter 2.
77. Cowell, *Kaṇṇḍina-Jātaka*, story no. 13.
78. Cowell, *Takka-Jātaka*, story no. 63. Already referred to in detail in Chapter 2.
79. Cowell, *Mora-Jātaka*, story no. 159.
80. Cowell, *Anabhirati-Jātaka*, story no. 185.
81. Cowell, *Valāhassa-Jātaka*, story no. 196.
82. Cowell, *Sayha-Jātaka*, story no. 310.
83. Cowell, *Ananusociya-Jātaka*, story no. 328.
84. Cowell, *Mahā-Paduma-Jātaka*, story no. 472.
85. Cowell, *Mudulakkhaṇa-Jātaka*, story no. 66.
86. Cowell, *Culla-Bodhi-Jātaka*, story no. 443.
87. Cowell, *Kuddāla-Jātaka*, story no. 70.
88. Cowell, *Kuhaka-Jātaka*, story no. 89.
89. Davids, *Psalms of the Early Buddhists*, canto 5, commentary XLI, verse 82–6.
90. Ibid., canto 1, part 10, commentary XCIX, verse 99.
91. Ibid., canto 1, part 12, commentary CXVIII, verse 118.
92. Ibid., canto 2, part 3, commentary CXLVI, verse 171–2.
93. Oldenberg and Pischel, *Thera- and Theri-gatha*, verse 171–2, http://

gretil.sub.uni-goettingen.de/gretil/2_pali/1_tipit/2_sut/5_khudd/theragou.htm.

94. Davids, *Psalms of the Early Buddhists*, canto 3, commentary CLXXXI, verse 252–4.
95. Ibid., canto 4, commentary CLXXXIX, verse 279–82.
96. See Chapter 2.
97. Cowell, *Keli-Sīla-Jātaka*, story no. 202.
98. See story no. 306.
99. Cowell, *Indasamānagotta-Jātaka*, story no. 161.
100. Cowell, *Maṇi-Kaṇṭha-Jātaka*, story no. 253.
101. See story no. 78.
102. Cowell, *Mahāsuka-Jātaka*, story no. 429.
103. See story no. 223.
104. Cowell, *Cakka-Vāka-Jātaka*, story no. 451.
105. Cowell, *Anusāsika-Jātaka*, story no. 115.
106. He is identified in the story as a delicately nurtured ksatriya and a Buddha. I believe this to be the title given to a person based on their possession of supernatural powers.
107. Cowell, *Cullasuka-Jātaka*, story no. 430.
108. Davids, *Psalms of the Early Buddhists*, canto 1, part 3, commentary XXX, verse 30.
109. Cowell, *Pānīya-Jātaka*, story no. 459.
110. See story no. 102.
111. Cowell, *Chaddanta-Jātaka*, story no. 514.
112. A prerequisite quality in a woman whose marriage is being arranged.
113. Davids, *Psalms of the Early Buddhists*, canto 1, part 3, commentary XXV, verse 25.
114. Ibid., canto 1, part 2, commentary XIV, verse 14.
115. Cowell, *Sālikedāra-Jātaka*, story no. 484.
116. See story no. 417.
117. Davids, *Psalms of the Early Buddhists*, canto 6, commentary LII, verse 139–44.
118. Ibid., canto 12, commentary LXV, verse LXV.
119. Ibid., canto 2, part 1, commentary CXXX, verse 139–40.
120. As discussed in Chapter 2.
121. Cowell, *Neru-Jātaka*, story no. 379.
122. See story no. 62.
123. Cowell, *Lomahaṁsa-Jātaka*, story no. 94.

124. Cowell, *Sigāla-Jātaka*, story no. 113.
125. Devadatta was a cousin of the Buddha. He had a different group of followers from the Buddha, but was envious of the latter. In many stories, his hostile presence against the Buddhist saṇgha is evident.
126. Cowell, *Kurunga-Miga-Jātaka*, story no. 206.
127. Cowell, *Bharu-Jātaka*, story no. 213.
128. Cowell, *Kāsāva-Jātaka*, story no. 221.
129. Cowell, *Nigrodha-Jātaka*, story no. 445.
130. Cowell, *Khaṇḍahāla-Jātaka*, story no. 542.
131. Cowell, *Mahāpiṅgala-Jātaka*, story no. 240.
132. See story no. 96.
133. Cowell, *Susīma-Jātaka*, story no. 163.
134. Cowell, *Mahilāmukha-Jātaka*, story no. 26.
135. See story no. 320.
136. Cowell, *Santhava-Jātaka*, story no. 162.
137. See story no. 130.
138. Davids, *Psalms of the Early Buddhists*, canto 5, commentary XLII, verse 88–91.
139. See story no. 301.
140. Davids, *Psalms of the Early Buddhists*, canto 5, commentary XLVI, verse 107–11.
141. See story no. 318.
142. Davids, *Psalms of the Early Buddhists*, canto 1, part 9, commentary LXXXVIII, verse 88.
143. Ibid., canto 5, commentary XLIII, verse 93–6.
144. Ibid., canto 1, part 1, commentary II, verse 2.
145. See story no. 106.
146. Davids, *Psalms of the Early Buddhists*, canto 1, part 12, commentary CXIV, verse 114.
147. See story no. 211.
148. Cowell, *Tittira-Jātaka*, story no. 37.
149. Davids, *Psalms of the Early Buddhists*, canto 5, commentary CXCIX, verse 320–4.
150. Cowell, *Tittha-Jātaka*, story no. 25.
151. See story no. 327.
152. Davids, *Psalms of the Early Buddhists*, canto 1, part 2, commentary XI, verse 11.
153. Cowell, *Kañcanakkhandha-Jātaka*, story no. 56.
154. Cowell, *Sūkara-Jātaka*, story no. 153.

155. See story no. 374.
156. Cowell, *Kuṭidūsaka-Jātaka*, story no. 321.
157. See story no. 106.
158. Davids, *Psalms of the Early Buddhists*, canto 1, part 10, commentary CI, verse 101.
159. Cowell, *Saṁvara-Jātaka*, story no. 462.

Epilogue

A STUDY OF THE three texts of the *Khuddaka Nikāya* reveals different aspects of marriage. The varied narratives and verses are reflective of the dominant, contemporary voices of the society in which they were composed, located mainly around the Gangetic basin. These texts swirl together an unmistakably Buddhist ethos with the language of the masses. In this quest to learn about the past of gender relations it has been understood that sexuality is not given, it is produced. Sexuality is the linchpin of power relations. Matrimonial alliances are of great importance as they are closely tied to the economy. Marriage and the private sphere of the householder have always been deeply political spaces in society as it guaranteed the reproduction of endogamous castes. The fear evoked by women choosing their own partners brought about a series of measures of patriarchal control, as discussed on a number of occasions throughout this volume. The basic categorization scheme of Buddhist society closely paralleled the brāhmaṇical social order. Indeed, in the Buddhist traditions the landowning class—who came to be defined as the *gahapatis*—occupied the most significant position in the social ladder. Their paramount significance stemmed from their relation of patronage with the saṇgha. Uma Chakravarti suggests that the term *gahapati* evolved through the social context of the sixth century BCE.[1] The term which previously designated the head of the family came to stand for an economic category, a landowning class that owned large amounts of property. Gradually they became the most important lay followers of the Buddha. Their monetary assistance was vital to the Buddhist saṇgha. Against this backdrop the representation of the institution of marriage in relation to renunciation had far-reaching implications. Understanding the 'beyond' in marriage encompasses several areas in the socio-economic sphere. It allows us to discuss numerous aspects of human relations and permits us to explore other possibilities that the Buddhist textual evidence constantly tried to frame as alternatives to the life of a householder.

In this volume, an attempt has been made to initiate a dialogue by interrogating the numerous commonalities as well as differences present in the Buddhist sources. Through the representation of marriage in the textual traditions, the depiction of social stratification in the Buddhist textual evidence has been closely examined. A clear understanding of the brāhmaṇical model of social division and the Buddhist response to it becomes apparent in every portrayal of social existence in the texts. Chakravarti's thought-provoking argument[2] encouraged me to reorganize my understanding of caste and class divisions in the Buddhist tradition. I agree with her views regarding social stratification and was compelled to highlight the grey zones in the representations of discrimination of common folk as far the textual evidence permitted. The texts that I used share certain commonalities despite their chronological variations. They were developed over centuries and rested on Buddhist philosophical ideals in general. However, unlike the *Vinaya Piṭaka*, the doctrinal references to the Buddhist ethos are not prominent in these texts. On the one hand the everyday experiences of common people recorded in this textual genre illustrate the pragmatic aspect of the social categorization in the period through which the texts developed. On the other, the strong Buddhist control over the compilation of the texts explains the Buddhist way of perceiving the same. The commentaries and *gāthās* are important to the structural framework of the Jātakas, the *Therīgāthā* and the *Theragāthā*. This allows us to compare the content of the *gāthās* and commentaries in each case. From this, a clear idea of deliberate inclusion and exclusion comes to light. For instance, in the verse of each of the *therīs*, apart from their past experiences in their worldly existence, an account of their encounter with the Master and the experience of liberation is manifested. This can be contrasted with the *Theragāthā* where the verses deal with the *theras* description of their life as recluses. We derive an idea about their lineage and past life only from the commentaries on the verses.

From the above two instances it becomes apparent that the past lineage of the *theras* and *therīs* were contained in the commentaries if not the verses. On the one hand this is indicative of a deliberate process of inclusion of the past records of the recluses in order to emphasize that the universalist doctrine of the Buddha was open to all. Admission to the order was not restricted to any particular category. Juxtaposing these two conflicting ideas makes it clear that the Buddhist ethos was structured on multiple factors in the social world on which the saṇgha depended for its maintenance. In the Jātakas, however, we come across a different situation. Each of the *gāthās* is contextualised by a narrative. However, the difference in content is striking. The narratives give a detailed understanding of the context and the characters involved, whereas the *gāthās*, very uniquely, intend to convey Buddhist values in an ironic way to the audiences concerned.

In negotiating matrimonial alliances the categorization of people into high and low strata in the Buddhist texts becomes quite explicit. It is evident that the Buddhist ethos did not challenge the hierarchical division in the social sphere based on class and caste differences. Often, the usage of animal motifs further confirms this. Certain groups of animals indicating a 'lower' status often bear similarities with the 'lower' section of society and the animals in the 'higher' groups serve the same purpose in the human world.

A contrasting situation crops up in the representations of renunciation where the choice of renouncing the world and attaining the highest goal of the Buddhist tradition was never restricted to any particular section of the society. However, the *gahapati*, represented as the householder and sincerely supporting the saṇgha in the human world has been projected as an ideal. As Ranabir Chakravarti states, the Pālī canonical texts indicate the Buddhist way of referring to the sharply divided society outside the saṇgha. An alternative way of dividing the society into *ukkaṭṭha kula* (elite) and *hīna kula* (non-elites) in sharp contrast to the varṇa-divided society became operative.[3]

Another aspect of class difference occurs in the selection of the bride and groom by the parents. Marriages arranged between 'equal' categories were held to be ideal. This, once again, closely reflects the brāhmaṇical system of maintaining the purity of lineage through caste taboos. As in the brāhmaṇical tradition, women were categorized as the most vulnerable class who needed strict vigilance and control in order to assure the sanctity of their 'pure' bloodline. What one can observe is that although Buddhism never considered the caste of a person as important to enter the Order, endogamous marriages received more preference over other forms of marriage. This reveals the dichotomous attitude of Buddhism towards caste.

In many of the Jātakas we find descriptions of the strict surveillance over women especially in situations stemming out of marriage. This reveals the continuation of a brāhmaṇical precedent rather than a change which Buddhist principles championed. I would agree with the proposition of Chakravarti[4] that Buddhism hardly visualized a society without inequalities; instead, the changing society was conceived by the Buddha on more rational values. The Buddha paid greater value to the actual status of an individual than his ritual status in society.[5] Indeed, the king had a significant position in the social sphere. The *cakkavatti* (title bestowed on a noble king who is considered the ruler of the world) was imposed with a new role of maintaining order in a period of social transition. We have already seen how the king could independently choose his conjugal partner and also decide the ideal moment for him to renounce worldly life. In both instances he stood in contrast to the rest of society where marriage or entry to the Order was hardly a choice made by the individual.

Undeniably, the textual evidence indicates a certain space of dissent for women. Like men they had access to the Buddhist religious path; however, this was mediated through certain restrictions. The unprecedented evidence of learned women attaining the status of a teacher features prominently in the verses of the nuns. Although marriage was not sacrosanct in the Buddhist texts the vulnerable condition of an unmarried woman was acknowledged. She was not liable to be trusted or left alone. Besides, fathers being keen on the virginity of their daughters as a precondition to good matchmaking was significant as mentioned repeatedly in the Jātakas. As the texts were developed over a huge time span, the repetition of such instances possibly hint at the prolonged existence of such practices in society. The absence of any such ordeal for men indicates the patriarchal bias of society.

Gerda Lerner[6] visualized class relations for men and women as completely different experiences. For men, class relations are based on the ownership of the means of production. On the contrary, for women, class is mediated through their sexual relationship to a man. Instances supporting this notion are not rare in the Buddhist textual traditions.

Evidence from the Jātakas suggests that class relations for women depended on their ties to men, while developments in the *Therīgāthā* presents a different picture. A constant emphasis on the upward social mobility of women through the means of donating to the Buddhist saṇgha becomes significant in this context and clearly hints at their independent access to wealth. However, we cannot presume that the widespread idea of independent women in the Buddhist texts points to an egalitarian society. At most it can be said that the *Therīgāthā* catered to an audience which included women who had access to wealth. Even if some of them were not well off, they had independent minds to look beyond patriarchal limitations. This makes me agree with Kathryn R. Blackstone's[7] theory that the verses of the *Therīgāthā* were authored by women.

In most of the Jātaka narratives, attempts to humanize female characters and present them in diverse roles—portraying their agency, rage, liberty and empathy—reflects the text's intent in detail and the finesse of society in particular. The Jātakas include the portrayal of courtesans as rebellious women and the *Therīgāthā* portray *bhikkhunis* as women who suffered in the worldly life and, thus, could severe this bond and join the saṇgha as an alternative. Courtesans often used their agency to retaliate against social norms. They were not portrayed as helpless and cowardly. The rage embodied by many female characters shows their power to challenge the misogynist society. In a story from the Jātakas (discussed earlier in this volume), a father followed an unusual method to test the virginity of his daughter before arranging her marriage. This story is terrible and disturbing at many levels. The daughter is not only treated as a mere object but an extension of the family's honour. This mirrors the idea on which the entire idea of rape is based—which is often used as a tool to rid a rival 'other' of their honour. The Jātakas had a clear intention of influencing lay society. Therefore, the representations and voices of women in the stories are worth analysing. However, in contrast to the strong-willed courtesans, often woman characters who are outspoken and express their infatuation and sexuality are marred and villified. This stems from the idea that women with agency and will are intimidating. At times, animal characters are deployed to represent the idea. For instance, in a Jātaka narrative the evil nature of exogamous marriages has been subtly portrayed through the character of the lioness. She has been described as dangerous, vocal and intimidating, and as one who had to be avoided by all means.

Another aspect of gender relations is observed in many stories where Buddha asked his disciples to discipline unruly wives through physical assault. This actually glorifies the sheer display of chauvinism and the act of inflicting violence on women. In the chapters of this volume I have also tried to discuss the operation of individual choice in constituting marital ties as well as the nature of choice made by the recluse in opting out of those ties. What is interesting about these narratives is the fact that in most instances marriage was more of a practice and was considered a natural stage in the life of an individual. We saw that marriage was systematically arranged within families of equal status. Anything 'beyond' this paradigm was looked down upon as a transgression. Yet, certain accommodations could be made in such instances in place of strict exclusion from the social order. For instance, eloping couples might not be accepted by their parents, but children born out of those unions had a certain degree of acceptance. Perhaps this indicated the inclusive tendency of the Buddhist ethos. Besides, 'beyond' the social world, the world of liberation served as a viable alternative to worldly suffering. Entry to the saṇgha was not always a natural choice for the individual. At times, the Buddha played a strong, influential role in inspiring the recluse to sever ties with worldly attachments. Paradoxically, parents forcing their children into marriage were no fewer than instances of parents encouraging their children to enter the Buddhist saṇgha. What can be said in way of conclusion is that the social mosaic of the time reflected in the textual evidence can best be understood in terms of multiple possibilities. A number of attitudes become apparent from the narratives. The juxtaposition of patriarchal values, gender bias and the inclusiveness of the Buddhist tradition are visible time and again in all three texts of the Buddhist traditions that have been examined.

So what can we finally take away from the Buddhist narratives about the history of gender relations and the intentions of the texts? What we learn is certainly different from what the narratives want us to imbibe. The narratives probably want us to internalize and normalize the passivity and docility expected of a woman to make her acceptable and desirable. However, the fallen wives, rebellious courtesans, disgusted wives, and outspoken maidens teach us not to concede to patriarchal norms or hide as a victim. Instead, one should use one's agency and establish one's claim as an equal human being. A female recluse in the *Therīgāthā* successfully narrated the strength of will power in breaking shackles and embracing alternative structures to gain liberation. Buddhist popular narratives raised such issues much ahead of their time. Thus, it is of utmost importance to contemplate their relevance and impact in the present time as well.

NOTES

1. Uma Chakravarti, *Social Dimensions of Early Buddhism*, New Delhi: Munshiram Manoharlal, 1996, p. 84.
2. See Chapter 1 of this work.
3. Ranabir Chakravarti, *Exploring Early India: Upto c.AD 1300*, New Delhi: Primus Books, 2016, p. 115.
4. Ibid., p. 181.
5. Ibid., p. 116.
6. Gerda Lerner, *The Creation of Patriarchy*, New York and Oxford: Oxford University Press, 1986, p. 9.
7. Ibid., p. 6.

Bibliography

Primary Sources

Cowell, E.B., ed., *The Jātakas*, tr. Robert Chalmers, vol. 1, New Delhi: Munshiram Manohorlal, 2002.

———, ed., *The Jātakas*, tr. W.H.D. Rouse, vol. 2, New Delhi: Munshiram Manohorlal, 2002.

———, ed., *The Jātakas*, tr. H.T. Francis and R.A. Neil, vol. 3, New Delhi: Munshiram Manohorlal, 2002.

———, ed., *The Jātakas*, tr. W.H.D. Rouse, vol. 4, New Delhi: Munshiram Manohorlal, 2002.

———, ed., *The Jātakas*, tr. H.T. Francis, vol. 5, New Delhi: Munshiram Manoharlal, 2002.

———, ed., *The Jātakas*, tr. W.H.D. Rouse, vol. 6, New Delhi, Munshiram Manohorlal, 2002.

Fausboll, V., ed., *The Jātakas Together with its Commentaries*, vols. 1–6, London: Trubner & Co., 1877–96.

Hallisey, Charles, tr., *Therigatha: Poems of the First Buddhist Women*, London: Murty Classical Library of India, 2015.

Oldenberg, H. and R. Pischel, *The Thera- and Theri-gatha (Stanzas Ascribed to Elders of the Buddhist Order of Recluses)* (online version), London: Pali Text Society, 1883, see http://gretil.sub.uni-goettingen.de/gretil/2_pali/1_tipit/2_sut/5_khudd/theragou.htm, accessed 10 April 2016.

Rhys Davids, C.A.F., *Psalms of the Early Buddhists*, London: Pali Text Society, Luzac and Co. Ltd, 1964.

——— and T.W. William Stede, eds., *Pali English Dictionary*, Delhi: Motilal Banarsidass, 2003.

Secondary Sources

Altekar, A.S., *The Position of Women in Hindu Civilization: From Prehistoric Times to the Present Day*, New Delhi: Motilal Banarsidass, 2005.

Appadurai, A., F.J. Koro and M. Mills, eds., *Gender, Genre and Power in South Asian Expressive Traditions*, New Delhi: Motilal Banarsidass, 1994.

Bailey, Grey and Ian Mabbett, eds., *The Sociology of Early Buddhism*, New York: Cambridge University Press, 2003.

Beauvoir, Simone de, *The Second Sex*, London: Vintage Classics, 1997.

Bhattacharji, Sukumari, *Women and Society in Ancient India*, Calcutta: Basumati, 1994.

Bhattacharya, Sabyasachi ed., *Approaches to History: Essays in Indian Historiography*, New Delhi: Primus Books, 2011.

Blackstone, Kathryn R., *Women in the Footsteps of the Buddha: Struggle for Liberation in the Therīgāthā*, New Delhi: Motilal Banarsidass, 2000.

Bopearachchi, Osmund and Suchandra Ghosh, eds., *Early Indian History and Beyond: Essays in Honour of B.D. Chattopadhyaya*, New Delhi: Primus Books, 2019.

Cabezon, Jose Ignacio, ed., *Buddhism, Sexuality, and Gender*, New Delhi: Sri Satguru Publications, 1992.

Chakravarti, Ranabir, *Exploring Early India: Upto c.AD 1300*, New Delhi: Primus Books, 2016.

Chakravarti, Uma, *The Social Dimensions of Early Buddhism*, New Delhi: Munshiram Manoharlal, 1996.

———, *Everyday Lives, Everyday Histories: Beyond the Kings and Brahmanas of 'Ancient' India*, New Delhi: Tulika Books, 2006.

———, *Gendering Caste through a Feminist Lens*, Kolkata: Stree, 2006.

———, 'The Jātaka as Popular Tradition', in *Cultural History of Early South Asia: A Reader*, ed. Shonaleeka Kaul, New Delhi: Orient BlackSwan, 2014.

Chandra, Moti, *The World of Courtesans*, New Delhi: Vikas Publishing House, 1973.

Chattopadhyaya, Brajadulal, *Studying Early India: Archaeology, Texts and Historical Issues*, New Delhi: Permanent Black, 2003.

Collett, Alice, ed., *Women in Early Buddhism: Comparative Textual Studies*, New York: Oxford University Press, 2014.

Feer, M.L., *A Study of the Jātakas*, Calcutta: Susil Gupta, 1964.

Fick, Richard, *The Social Organisation in North-East India in Buddha's Time*, tr. S.K. Maitra, Calcutta: University of Calcutta, 1920.

Geetha, V., *Gender: Theorizing Feminism*, Kolkata: Stree, 2002.

———, *Patriarchy*, Kolkata: Stree, 2007.

Ghosh, Anindita, ed., *Behind the Veil: Resistance, Women and the Everyday in Colonial South East Asia,* New Delhi: Permanent Black, 2007.

Gombrich, Richard, *Theravāda Buddhism: A Social History from Ancient Benares to Modern Colombo*, London: Routledge and Kegan Paul, 2006.

Granoff, Phyllis, 'Karma, Curse, or Divine Illusion: The Destruction of the Buddha's Clan and the Slaughter of the Yādavas', in *Epic and Argument in Sanskrit Literary History*, ed. Sheldon Pollock, New Delhi: Manohar, 2010.

Gross, Rita M., *Buddhism after Patriarchy: A Feminist History, Analysis and Reconstruction of Buddhism*, Delhi: Sri Satguru Publications, 1995.

Holmes, Mary, *What is Gender? Sociological Approaches*, London: Sage, 2007.

Horner, I.B., *Women under Primitive Buddhism*, New Delhi: Motilal Banarsidass, 1990.

Jamison, Stephanie W., 'Women "Between the Empires" and "Between the Lines"' in *Between the Empires: Society in India 300 BCE to 400 CE*, ed. Patrick Olivelle, New York: Oxford University Press, 2007.

John, Mary E., ed., *Women's Studies in India: A Reader*, New Delhi: Penguin, 2008.

Jones, John G., *Tales and Teachings of the Buddha*, Christchurch, New Zealand: Cybereditions Corporation, 2001.

Kaul, Shonaleeka, *Imagining the Urban: Sanskrit and the City in Early India*, New Delhi: Permanent Black, 2010.

———, ed., *Cultural History of Early South Asia: A Reader*, New Delhi: Orient BlackSwan, 2014.

King, Anna and Killinley Dermot, eds., *Religions of South Asia*, London: Equinox Publishing, 2012.

Kosambi, D.D., *Myth and Reality*, Bombay: Popular Prakashan, 2013.

———, *An Introduction to the Study of Indian History*, Bombay: Popular Prakashan, 1999.

Kosambi, Meera, *Crossing Thresholds: Feminist Essays in Social History*, Ranikhet: Permanent Black, 2007.

Lal, Malashri and Namita Gokhale, eds., *In Search of Sita: Revisiting Mythology*, New Delhi: Yatra Books, 2009.

Law, B.C., ed., *Buddhistic Studies*, New Delhi: Low Price Publication, 2004.

Lerner, Gerda, *The Creation of Patriarchy*, New York: Oxford University Press, 1986.

Leslie, Julia, ed., *Roles and Rituals for Hindu Women*, New Delhi: Motilal Banarsidass, 1992.

Leslie, Julia and Mary McGee, eds., *Invented Identities: The Interplay of Gender, Religion and Politics in India*, New Delhi: Oxford University Press, 2000.

Malhan, Tara Sheemar, *Plunging the Ocean: Courts, Castes and Courtesans in the Kathāsaritsāgara*, New Delhi: Primus Books, 2017.

Menon, Nivedita, *Seeing Like a Feminist*, New Delhi: Penguin, 2012.

Misra, G.S.P., *The Age of Vinaya*, New Delhi: Munshiram Manoharlal, 1972.

Norman, K.R., *Pali Literature*, Wiesbaden: Otto Harrassowitz,1983.

Olivelle Patrick, ed., *Between the Empires: Society in India, 300 BCE to 400 CE*, New York: Oxford University Press, 2007.

———, tr., *Life of the Buddha by Ashvaghosha*, New York: New York University Press and the J.J.C. Foundation, 2008.

Pollock, Sheldon, ed., *Literary Cultures in History: Reconstructions from South Asia*, Berkely: University of California Press, 2003.

———, ed., *Epic and Argument in Sanskrit Literary History*, New Delhi: Manohar Publishers and Distributors, 2010.

Rhys Davids, T.W., *Buddhist India*, New Delhi, Munshiram Manoharlal, 1999.

Roy, Kumkum, ed., *Women in Early Indian Societies*, New Delhi: Manohar, 1999.

———, 'Recent Writings on Gender Relations in Early India', in *History and Gender: Some Explorations*, ed. Kirit K. Shah, Jaipur and New Delhi: Rawat Publications, 2005.

———, *The Power of Gender and the Gender of Power: Explorations in Early Indian History*, New Delhi: Oxford University Press, 2010.

———, ed., *Insights and Interventions: Essays in Honour of Uma Chakravarti*, Delhi: Primus Books, 2011.

———, ed., *Looking Within, Looking Without: Exploring Households in the Subcontinent through Time*, New Delhi: Primus Books, 2015.

———, *Gender and Early Textual Traditions*, Tripunithura, Kerala: Govt. Sanskrit College, 2015.

———, 'Negotiating Inequalities: Reflecting on the Early Buddhist Saṁgha', in *Studies in People's History*, vol. 3, no. 1, 2016, pp. 2–12.

Sahgal Smita, *Niyoga: Alternative Mechanism to Lineage Perpetuation in Early India: A Socio-Historical Enquiry*, New Delhi: Primus Books, 2017.

Sahu, Bhairabi Prasad, *The Changing Gaze: Regions and the Constructions of Early India*, New Delhi: Oxford University Press, 2013.

Sangari, K. and Uma Chakravarti, eds., *From Myths to Markets: Essays on Gender*, New Delhi: Manohar, 1999.

Schober, Juliane, ed., *Sacred Biography in the Buddhist Traditions of South and Southeast Asia*, New Delhi: Motilal Banarsidass, 2002.

Schopen, Gregory, *Figments and Fragments of Mahāyāna Buddhism in India*, Hawaii: University of Hawaii Press, 2005.

Shah, Kirit K., ed., *History and Gender: Some Explorations*, New Delhi and Jaipur: Rawat Publications, 2005.

Shah, Shalini, *The Making of Womanhood: Gender Relations in the Mahābhārata*, New Delhi: Manohar, 2012.

———, *Love, Eroticism and Female Sexuality in Classical Sanskrit Literature, 7th to 13th Centuries*, New Delhi: Manohar, 2009.

Sponberg, Alan, 'Attitudes Toward Women and the Feminine in Early Buddhism', in *Buddhism, Sexuality and Gender*, ed. Jose Ignacio Cabezon, New Delhi: Sri Satguru Publications, 1992.

Talim, Meena, *Woman in Early Buddhist Literature*, Bombay: University of Bombay Press, 1972.

Thapar, Romila, *From Lineage to State: Social Formation in the Mid-first Millennium* BC *in the Ganga Valley*, New Delhi: Oxford University Press, 2006.

———, *Ancient Indian Social History: Some Interpretations*, New Delhi: Orient BlackSwan, 2010.

Thapar, Romila, *Cultural Pasts: Essays in Early Indian History*, New Delhi: Oxford University Press, 2000.

———, *Early India from the Origins to* AD *1300*, New Delhi: Penguin, 2003.

———, *Śakuntalā: Texts, Readings, Histories*, New York: Columbia University Press, 2011.

———, *Aśoka and the Decline of the Mauryas*, New Delhi: Oxford University Press, 2012.

———, *The Past Before Us: Historical Traditions of Early North India*, New Delhi: Permanent Black, 2013.

———, *Readings in Early Indian History*, New Delhi: Oxford University Press, 2013.

———, *The Past as Present: Forging Contemporary Identities through History*, New Delhi: Aleph Book Co., 2014.

Wagle, Narendra, *Society at the Time of the Buddha*, Bombay: Popular Prakashan, 1995.

Warder, A.K., *Indian Buddhism*, New Delhi: Motilal Banarsidass, 2008.
Winternitz, Maurice, *History of Indian Literature: Buddhist Literature and Jaina Literature*, New Delhi: Oriental Books, 1977.

Index